Study Guide for Book Clubs: Pachinko

KATHRYN COPE

CONTENTS

INTRODUCTION

There are few things more rewarding than getting together with a group of like-minded people and discussing a good book. Book club meetings, at their best, are vibrant, passionate affairs. Each member will bring along a different perspective and ideally there will be heated debate.

A surprising number of book club members, however, report that their meetings have been a disappointment. Even though their group loved the particular book they were discussing, they could think of astonishingly little to say about it. Failing to find interesting discussion angles for a book is the single most common reason for book group discussions to fall flat. Most book groups only meet once a month and a lackluster meeting is frustrating for everyone.

Study Guides for Book Clubs were born out of a passion for reading groups. Packed with information, they take the hard work out of preparing for a meeting and ensure that your book group discussions never run dry. How you choose to use the guides is entirely up to you. The author biography, historical, and style sections provide useful background information which may be interesting to share with your group at the beginning of your meeting. The all-important list of discussion questions, which will probably form the core of your meeting, can be found towards the end of this guide. To support your responses to the discussion questions, you may find it helpful to refer to the 'Themes' and 'Character' sections.

A detailed plot synopsis is provided as an aide-memoire if you need to recap on the finer points of the plot. There is also a quick quiz - a fun way to test your knowledge and bring your discussion to a close. Finally, if this was a book that you particularly enjoyed, the guide concludes with a list of books similar in style or subject matter.

This guide contains spoilers. Please do not be tempted to read it before you have read the original novel as plot surprises will be well and truly ruined.

Kathryn Cope, 2018

MIN JIN LEE

Min Jin Lee was born in Seoul, South Korea. In 1976, when she was seven, her parents emigrated to Queens, New York. The move represented a significant change in lifestyle for her father and mother, who had respectively worked in marketing and as a music teacher in Korea. Initially opening a news kiosk, they progressed to running a small wholesale jewellery shop and were eventually successful enough to send their three daughters to college. Lee graduated from Yale in 1990 with a degree in history. She went to law school and practiced law for two years before giving up to become a full-time writer. Her debut novel, *Free Food for Millionaires* was published in 2007. A coming-of-age tale, it tells the story of Casey Han, the daughter of Korean immigrants who grows up in Queens but is increasingly attracted by a glitzy Manhattan lifestyle. Critically acclaimed, the novel was a National Book Award finalist.

Although *Pachinko* was Lee's second published novel, she began it before *Free Food for Millionaires* in the 1990s. Her decision to write about the experience of Koreans in Japan was inspired by a talk she attended in the 1990s. Having grown up in the USA where Koreans were generally perceived as aspirational and hardworking, she was shocked to learn that, in Japan, they were treated as second-class citizens. Lee's early attempts at the novel (then entitled *Motherland*) proved frustratingly unsuccessful. Beginning her story in the 1970s, she focused the narrative on Solomon Baek (a character who would eventually appear in the final third of *Pachinko*). Somehow, however, the story did not feel authentic. It was only when Lee's husband (a Japanese banker) took a job in Tokyo that the book began to come together. Living in Japan from 2007–2011, Min Jin Lee had the opportunity to interview the Koreans who lived there. As a result, she realised that she would have to delve further back in history (1910, to be exact) to do their story justice. *Pachinko* was finally published in 2017. A National

Book Award finalist, it became a *New York Times* Bestseller and appeared on over 70 best book of the year lists.

In addition to her novels, Min Jin Lee has written short fiction, literary criticism and pieces on politics, culture, travel and food. These have been widely published in a range of international publications including *The New Yorker*, *The New York Times Book Review*, *The Times*, *The Guardian*, and *Conde Nast Traveler of London*.

The author currently lives in Boston and is working on *American Hagwon* which she has described as the third in her Korean trilogy.

HISTORICAL CONTEXT

For readers with little knowledge of twentieth century Korean history, *Pachinko* provides a wealth of information. Spanning the period from Korea's colonisation by Japan through the Second World War and the Korean War, Lee reconstructs the recent history of the Korean people. The thorough nature of the author's historical research is clear in her detailed descriptions of everything from living conditions in traditional Korean homes to the cramped layouts of the Japanese ghettoes and the interiors of pachinko parlours.

It is a mark of Lee's great skill as a writer that she applies her extensive research with a light touch. Cultural details are unobtrusively slipped in through the course of the story without ever slowing down the plot. By sharing the routines of her characters, readers learn, for example, that Japanese houses are divided into rooms by sliding paper doors and measured by mats. We also discover that it is routine for Japanese residents to visit public bathhouses to perform their daily ablutions. Immersing readers in the world of her characters, Lee offers no lengthy explanations and even includes Korean and Japanese words, trusting our ability to decipher them.

Pachinko shows rather than tells the history of the Korean people by illustrating how historical and national events affect the characters on a personal level. The economic impact of Japan's occupation of Korea is shown first through Hoonie's parents, who rent their bedroom to lodgers to pay increasingly exorbitant taxes. Yangjin's father is forced to marry her off when his farmland is taken over by the Japanese and he can no longer afford to feed his daughters. Meanwhile, the effects of the Japanese rice shortage in 1918 are illustrated when Yangjin struggles to buy white rice to celebrate Sunja's wedding as all available supplies have been reserved for the Japanese.

When Sunja and Isak move to Japan, the discrimination Koreans face there is illustrated in the miserable living conditions of Yoseb and Kyunghee. The religious persecution of Christians by the Japanese is also powerfully demonstrated when Isak and his associates are imprisoned indefinitely. As Japan enters into World War II, Lee shows the impact on the ordinary man as prices are raised, food becomes scarce and Yoseb cannot support his family even with two jobs. When the war comes to an end, we again see the individual cost of this as Yoseb, who is working in a military factory, is horrifically burned in the nuclear bombing of Nagasaki.

During Sunja's years in Japan, she hears stories (largely from Hansu) about the terrible state of her homeland. These stories take on a reality when Hansu retrieves Yangjin from Korea, aged and clearly malnourished. Forced to give up the boarding house due to further raises in taxes, we learn that she has been working as a servant and sleeping in a cupboard. Meanwhile, Bokhee and Dokhee, have suffered the fate of many Korean girls and been lured into sexual slavery.

Pachinko illustrates that, even by the 1970s and 1980s, Japanese discrimination against Koreans had not come to an end. When Solomon goes through the humiliating process of applying for his alien registration card on his fourteenth birthday, Lee demonstrates that all Koreans born in Japan still had to apply for permission to stay there. By illustrating the ways in which her characters are affected by historical events, Lee ensures that these details stick in readers' minds.

While *Pachinko* conveys details of Korean history more powerfully than any factual account, the following provides a straightforward explanation of the novel's historical background.

The Japanese Occupation of Korea

Sandwiched between the larger powers of China, Russia and Japan, the geographical location of the Korean Peninsula made it ripe for colonisation. Russia and Japan fought for control of the country and, in 1910, Japan was victorious. Korea was promptly annexed and Japan installed a puppet leader (Emperor Sunjong). By the time the emperor died in 1926, Japan had done away with any pretence of maintaining the Korean Empire and was completely in control of the country.

Japanese rule had many consequences for Koreans. Economically they became invariably worse off as new land reforms were introduced. Korean landowners who could not provide written evidence of their ownership had their land confiscated and sold on to Japanese owners. Other landowners found they could not afford to invest in the irrigation improvements that Japanese law required them to make. As a consequence, many farmers became tenant farmers almost overnight and were made to hand over half their produce as rent. Meanwhile, Korean peasants were forced to pay crippling taxes leading to great hardship and causing even more of them to lose their properties. In some cases, the women of these families were forced into prostitution to make ends meet.

The colonial government's policy of squeezing the Koreans dry was illustrated during Japan's rice shortage in 1918. Lacking sufficient rice crops, Japan put pressure on Korea to increase their output. As the Korean peasants did so, however, they found they had less and less rice to eat themselves as it was all reserved for the Japanese.

In addition to introducing these economic hardships, the Japanese brought in regulations in the 1930s and 1940s that attempted to erode Korea's cultural identity. Koreans were issued with Japanese names and it became compulsory to worship at Shinto shrines (Shinto being the official religion of Japan). Christians were persecuted, and the Korean language was suppressed in favour of Japanese. Overall, Japanese rule equated to a drastic loss of human rights for the Korean people.

Korean Migration to Japan

Hundreds of thousands of Koreans migrated to Japan in the first half of the twentieth century. Some made the journey voluntarily, hoping to escape the deprivation they suffered in their homeland. With the breakout of the Second World War, others were recruited (or coerced) to fill the labour shortages in Japan caused by the conscription of Japanese men. Korean men contributed to the Japanese war effort by working in military factories, while some Korean women were tricked or forced into working in the Japanese military brothels. By the end of World War II, over two million

11

Koreans resided in Japan.

Despite encouraging Koreans to migrate to Japan during the war, the Japanese did not extend a warm welcome. Japanese landlords refused to rent decent properties to Koreans, forcing them to congregate in slums. Koreans also faced discrimination in the workplace. Many jobs were simply not available to them and those that were inevitably paid badly and often involved long hours and dangerous working conditions.

Faced with hostility and few options to better themselves, some Koreans looked to moneymaking schemes that were disreputable (or considered to be so by Japanese society). Becoming a *yakuza* (the Japanese version of a mob member) was one possibility. Many others took advantage of the popularity of pachinko—a pinball-like game which emerged in Japan in the late 1920s. Similar to slot machine arcades or casinos, pachinko parlours continued to spring up across the country and were usually owned and staffed by Koreans. One of the great attractions of pachinko was that it provided an opportunity to gamble in a country where gambling for cash was illegal. Pachinko parlours narrowly avoided breaking the law by avoiding directly handing out cash to winners. Instead, they gave out prizes or tokens which could be exchanged for cash nearby. Despite their shady reputation, pachinko parlours were tolerated by the Japanese police as they significantly contributed to the economy. By allowing Koreans to monopolise the business, the Japanese reaped the financial benefits while vilifying those who ran them.

The Liberation of Korea

In 1945, World War II came to an end for the Japanese when U.S. forces dropped atomic bombs on Hiroshima and Nagasaki. With Japan's surrender, their colonial rule over Korea also ended and allied forces occupied the Korean Peninsula.

After the liberation of their country, many Koreans who were living in Japan returned to their homeland. Others, however, had no homes to go back to and approximately 650,000 Koreans ended up staying in Japan. Now, however, they were no longer considered Japanese subjects and were required to register as alien residents. After the Korean War, they were also forced to choose between affiliation to North or South Korea (although many of them had left their homeland before the country was divided). This began years of ambiguity over the legal status of Koreans in Japan. Even second, third and fourth generation migrants were labelled "Zainichi" (meaning a foreign citizen staying in Japan) and the process of alien registration was only repealed in 1993.

The Japanese Caste System

To gain a better understanding of the discrimination Koreans have faced in Japan, it is helpful to know something about the country's history of rigid social hierarchy—which began with the Japanese caste system. Lee alludes to this in *Pachinko* by introducing socially ostracised Japanese characters who are considered to be *Burakumin*. This concept is a residue from the Japanese feudal caste system which was unashamedly discriminatory and prejudiced.

The four-tiered Japanese caste system was introduced in the late sixteenth century. Japanese citizens could fall into one of four hierarchical castes (samurai, farmer, artisan, or merchant)—all of which were hereditary. There were also, however, those considered so lowly that they were beneath the caste system completely. These social outcasts fell into the categories of *Hinin*, *Kawaramono* and *Eta*. The *Hinin* (meaning "not human") included vagrants, beggars, ex-convicts, and street cleaners. The *Kawaramono* (meaning "dry, the rivers") were so called because they resided on the banks of the rivers that could not be converted into rice paddies. *Eta* (literally "abundance of filth") worked in jobs that were considered impure within the Buddhist and Shinto belief systems. These were roles that were generally considered repellent due to their association with death (butchery, abattoir work, leather tanners, executioners etc.). *Eta* were expected to live in the areas "contaminated" by their work and could only marry within the same social strata. As with the "untouchables" in the Hindu caste system, *Eta* status was inherited from one generation to another and there was nothing an individual could do to rise above it.

In 1871 both the feudal and the caste system were abolished in Japan. Those who had previously fallen beneath the four tiers of the system were redefined as "*Burakumin*" (meaning "people of the village"). While this was admittedly a less insulting label, the term "village" really equated to "ghetto" and the definition still ensured that society could identify the descendants of former social outcasts. Discrimination against them continued (albeit with a new name) and *Burakumin* still found themselves living in the worst areas, barred from many professions and socially ostracised. Unsurprisingly, some were drawn to organised crime, becoming *yakuza*. In the 1970s it was discovered that a list of *Burakumin* names and addresses was secretly being sold to many Japanese employers to help them weed out job applicants. Although this practice, once exposed, became illegal it is believed that many people still buy this information (often to check if future son- or daughters-in-law are descended from social outcasts).

The Korean War Onwards

Once the Japanese had withdrawn from Korea at the end of World War II, the country was divided along the 38th parallel (a division which was initially intended to be temporary). South of this border, the Americans had control while, in the North, the Russians installed a communist government. In 1948 the divided territories were officially established as separate countries. South Korea became the Republic of Korea while North Korea was named the Democratic People's Republic of Korea. Both sides hoped that the country would eventually be reunified under their rule.

On June 25, 1950, soldiers from the North crossed the 38th parallel and took possession of much of the South, instigating the Korean war. The United Nations intervened, sending largely American troops to support the South Koreans. Meanwhile, Russia and China supported North Korea, sending arms and soldiers respectively.

On July 27, 1953, North Korea signed an armistice with the United States. Although this brought an end to the fighting, it did not technically end the Korean War as South Korea did not formally agree to a peace treaty. By this point, approximately 3 million people had been killed and neither side had achieved its goal. Korea remained divided at the 38th parallel.

The Korean War is sometimes referred to as "the Forgotten War" as, in the memory of the American public, it has been overshadowed by World War II and the Vietnam War. It is not, however, a conflict that Koreans are likely to forget. As well as the many lives lost, North Korea, in particular, was left devastated by bombings and the enthusiastic use of napalm on the part of U.S.

forces. Industry, agriculture, and transportation systems were wiped out while the North Korean capital, Pyongyang, was flattened by approximately 250,000 bombs. As a result, North Koreans came to view the U.S.'s military campaign as a form of genocide.

After the war, the United States provided aid to South Korea while North Korea reconstructed itself with the help of the USSR and China. South Korea was governed by a series of capitalist dictatorships before finally becoming a democracy. North Korea has remained a communist dictatorship where civil liberties are severely restricted. The two countries remain at odds, although not at war, with both regimes believing they should govern the whole of Korea.

PLOT SYNOPSIS

Prologue

BOOK 1—Gohyang/ Hometown— 1910-1933

In 1910, Japan annexes Korea and property rents are raised by the corrupt colonial government. In Yeongdo—a village in Busan, South Korea—a fisherman and his wife respond to the rent raises by sleeping in the anteroom of the kitchen and renting out their bedroom to lodgers.

Of the couple's three sons, only one has survived. Born with a cleft palate and a twisted foot, Hoonie has little chance of finding a bride. When her son is twenty-seven, Hoonie's mother receives a visit from the local matchmaker. The matchmaker reveals that a tenant farmer (who has lost his lease as a result of the government's new land surveys) is looking for a husband for his youngest daughter, Yangjin. As he cannot afford to keep her, he is prepared to allow Yangjin to marry Hoonie if the family can raise the bride price.

Hoonie marries fifteen-year-old Yangjin. Their first three children die in infancy but their fourth child, Sunja, survives. Hoonie dotes on his daughter, relieved that she has not inherited his deformity. When Sunja is thirteen Hoonie dies of tuberculosis.

November 1932

Yangjin continues to run the boarding house after her husband's death. One evening an elegantly dressed man arrives, exhausted after a long journey from Pyongyang. Baek Isak is on his way to Osaka in Japan to take up a position as Associate Pastor. Although Yangjin has no vacancies, she allows Isak to squeeze in with her other lodgers.

Sixteen-year-old Sunja has confessed to her mother that she is pregnant. She will not reveal the father's identity but makes it clear that he cannot marry her. Meanwhile, one of Yangjin's servants notices blood on Isak's pillow—a sign of tuberculosis. Afraid of infecting everyone else, Isak offers to leave. Knowing that he would not survive the journey, Yangjin insists he stays until he is better.

June 1932

The story flashes back to six months earlier when Sunja first makes the acquaintance of a wealthy fish broker—Koh Hansu. One day, on the way back from the market, Sunja is accosted by three Japanese schoolboys. After insulting her, one of the boys grabs her breasts and suggests to his friends that they should rape her. At this moment, Hansu intervenes, grabbing the boy and threatening to have him killed.

Sunja begins to secretly meet Hansu at the cove where she washes the laundry. After three months their friendship develops into a sexual relationship.

While Hansu is away on business in Japan, Sunja realises that she is pregnant. Eagerly awaiting her lover's return, she anticipates a marriage proposal. When he finally arrives and learns of her pregnancy, however, Hansu reveals that he already has a wife and three children in Japan. Promising that he will take care of Sunja and her child as if they are married, Hansu offers to buy her a house. Devastated, Sunja refuses his financial help and ends their affair.

November 1932

As Isak recovers from his illness, Yangjin tells him about Sunja's pregnancy. She confides her anxiety about the inevitable disgrace that Sunja and her illegitimate baby will face.

Isak visits a church in Busan and speaks to the pastor. Pastor Shin tells Isak that many Koreans are now afraid to attend services as the government discourages Christian worship. Isak tells the pastor about Sunja's pregnancy and reveals that he is thinking of marrying her to save her from disgrace. Pastor Shin asks Isak to bring Sunja and Yangjin to talk to him.

When Isak proposes to Sunja she accepts, agreeing to

accompany him to Osaka where he will take up his ministry. Pastor Shin marries the couple after questioning Sunja rather harshly. Heartbroken at the loss of her daughter, Yangjin sees Sunja and her new son-in-law onto the ferry. Before they leave, she gives Sunja two gold rings to sell in case of emergency and advises her to be a good wife to Isak.

Osaka, April 1933

When Isak and Sunja arrive in Japan, Isak's brother, Yoseb, greets them at the train station in Osaka. Although Yoseb is a factory foreman, he and his family live in Ikaino—a makeshift Korean ghetto. Yoseb explains that all the Koreans live there as the Japanese will not rent decent houses to them. He also warns Isak and Sunja not to mix with their Korean neighbours as they are likely to steal from them. Despite their cramped living quarters, Yoseb's wife, Kyunghee, welcomes them effusively.

Sunja and Isak sleep together as man and wife for the first time and Sunja makes up her mind that she will love her husband. Isak goes to the Hanguk Presbyterian Church where he is to become the associate minister. Meeting his colleagues, Pastor Yoo and Sexton Hu, he discovers that neither of them takes a salary and his own earnings will be meagre.

Sunja finds life in Japan difficult to adjust to. She struggles to get used to her Japanese name and notices that Japanese people look at her with contempt. Amazed at how expensive everything is, she also worries about their lack of financial contribution to the household as Yoseb and Kyunghee refuse to accept the little money that Isak earns. Sunja and Kyunghee become close friends, spending their days together cooking. Kyunghee dreams of having her own *kimchi* stall at the market but tells Sunja that her husband refuses to let her work.

Two men call on Kyunghee claiming that Yoseb took out a loan and has fallen behind with his payments. Knowing nothing about the debt, Kyunghee is unable to pay them. Sunja, however, tells the men to return shortly when she will have the money.

Sunja visits a Korean pawnbroker and, after much haggling, sells a gold pocket watch (a former gift from Hansu). Later, the two men return and take Kyunghee and Sunja to their boss. The Korean moneylender cancels the loan, telling them that Yoseb borrowed the money in February. The women realise that he must have borrowed the sum to pay for Isak and Sunja's passage to Japan.

Yoseb is furious when he learns that his wife and sister-in-law have paid off the loan. He storms out of the house and does not return that night. Meanwhile, Sunja goes into labour and has a healthy baby boy. When Yoseb returns in the morning, Isak placates his brother by asking him to choose a name for the baby. Yoseb names him Noa.

BOOK 2 — Motherland — 1939-1962

Osaka, 1939

Six years later, Japan has allied itself to Germany in World War II and Sunja has had another baby—Mozasu.

One day Yoseb gets home from work to find the house empty. He goes to Isak's church and the worshippers tell him that Isak, Pastor Yoo and Sexton Hu have been arrested at a Shinto shrine. All Koreans are required to publicly bow to Shinto shrines and Sexton Hu had been caught mouthing the Lord's Prayer as he did so. When challenged, Hu declared that he was no longer prepared to worship an idol and all three men were taken to the police station.

Yoseb goes to the police station where the rest of his family are already congregated. He tries to convince the officer on duty that his brother is not involved in politics and that his health will not withstand prison. His words fall on deaf ears.

Although Isak is not allowed visitors in prison, Sunja takes in food every day in the hope that he will receive it. Unsure of what her future now holds, she decides to work as a peddler at the market. Yoseb protests but finally agrees that Kyunghee can make *kimchi* (Korean pickles) for the market and Sunja can sell them.

Sunja receives a hostile reception from fellow hawkers but eventually finds a spot by the train station next to the foul-smelling stall of a pork butcher. At first, she is intimidated but is soon able to sell as much *kimchi* as she and Kyunghee can make. Much of the money she earns, she saves for her sons' education.

One day Sunja is approached at the market by Kim Changho who runs a nearby restaurant. He tells her that the reputation of her *kimchi* has spread and he wants to buy as much as she can make for his restaurant. Sunja and Kyunghee devote themselves to making large quantities of the pickle. At school, Noa is teased as his clothes smell of *kimchi* spices. The teacher makes him sit with the Korean children whose families keep pigs in their home.

With their first large batch of *kimchi* made, Kyunghee and Sunja visit Kim Changho's restaurant. Kim offers the women jobs making *kimchi* and side dishes in the restaurant kitchen. The salary greatly exceeds the amount they can make at the market.

Kyunghee asks Yoseb's permission to take the job. He is horrified at the prospect but knows that he is unable to provide for the family alone, even with two full-time jobs. Japan's participation in the war has caused rapid inflation, raising prices to an exorbitant level.

May 1942

After two years, Isak is still in prison. With the income that Sunja and Kyunghee receive from the restaurant, however, the family's financial situation has improved.

Noa works hard at school and, unbeknown to his family, chooses to go by his Japanese name. One day he returns from school to find a dirty, emaciated man collapsed on the kitchen floor. Assuming that the man is a beggar, Noa gives him a coin and only recognises his father when he speaks.

Isak's captivity has left him weak, feverish and covered in scars from where he has been beaten. Sunja sends for a pharmacist who tells them that nothing can be done. Despite his pitiful state, Isak is glad to be reunited with his wife, brother and sons before he dies.

December 1944

With food in short supply in Japan, Kim Changho tells Sunja and Kyunghee that the restaurant will close until the war is over. Kyunghee accompanies Kim to the market and, while Sunja is alone in the restaurant, Koh Hansu arrives. Hansu explains that he owns the restaurant and that Kim Changho is his employee. He tells Sunja that he traced her eleven years ago when she sold his pocket watch, as the pawnbroker tried to sell it on to him. Knowing that Sunja would need money while Isak was in prison, he created the job in the restaurant for her.

Hansu tells Sunja that she must leave Osaka as he is certain that the Americans will be bombing the city in the next few days. He has already made arrangements for Kim Changho to take Sunja and the rest of her family to a farm outside Osaka. Sunja expresses doubt over whether she can convince Yoseb to abandon his house. Hansu replies that, if necessary, she must leave her in-laws behind as her priority must be to save her sons. Sunja asks Hansu if he can use his contacts to find out if her mother is safe in Korea.

Later the same day, Yoseb accepts a job offer at a steel factory in Nagasaki. When Sunja learns that the job offers excellent pay but Yoseb cannot take his family she realises that Hansu is behind it. That night, Kim Changho takes the women and boys to the farm while Yoseb leaves for Nagasaki. A few months later Osaka is devastated by bombings.

Tamaguchi (the owner of the potato farm) immediately puts the family to work and is delighted at how productive they are. After four months, Hansu arrives at the farm with Sunja's mother, who he has traced and brought over from Korea. He announces that, when the war is over, he will buy them a home and give Sunja money to educate the boys. Sunja refuses his offer insisting that she will continue to work in order to care for them.

The war ends when Nagasaki is bombed by the Americans. Yoseb is badly injured in the attack and Hansu's men locate him in a hospital. When Yoseb is brought to the farm, Kyunghee is shocked by how badly disfigured her husband's face is. Hansu provides medication to ease his pain.

Noticing the physical resemblance between Hansu and Noa, Yoseb realises the truth about Noa's parentage. When Hansu admits that he is Noa's father, Yoseb says that he must cut all contact with Noa before the boy realises who he is. Yoseb also declares that now the war is over, he plans to return to Korea to be with his parents. Alarmed at the thought of Sunja returning to Korea with his son, Hansu deceives Yoseb and Kyunghee claiming that, like many other Korean land owners, their parents have been killed. Hansu tells twelve-year-old Noa that, if he wants to return to school, they must go back to Osaka immediately.

Osaka 1949

The family return to Osaka to find that Yoseb's house has been destroyed by bombing. They rebuild the property and the women bring in an income by selling confectionery at the market. As Yoseb is so frail, Kim Changho continues to live with the family. The close proximity to Kyunghee is tortuous for him, however, as he is in love with her. He tells Hansu that, now that Korea is no longer under Japanese rule, he wishes to return to the North. Hansu pays for a prostitute to distract Kim Changho.

Osaka, January 1953

Noa has finished high school and is working as a bookkeeper. Hoping to go to Waseda University, he also studies for entrance examinations which he fails on his first attempt. Sunja and Kyunghee try to find ways to earn more so that Noa can give up his job and study full time. This proves difficult as Yoseb remains in poor health and his medical bills are expensive. Nevertheless, Yoseb continues to insist that Sunja should not accept money from Hansu for Noa's education.

Thirteen-year-old Mozasu is behind with his schooling and is placed in a class of ten-year-olds. He responds to the taunts of his Japanese classmates with his fists. One day a boy called Haruki Totoyama joins the class. Although Haruki is Japanese, he is poor and there are rumours that he is a *buraka* (from the lowest Japanese social class). Haruki is fatherless, and his younger brother has a mental disability which many people interpret as a curse. He tries to fit in, but the other children shun him. After seeing Haruki rejected on numerous occasions Mozasu, takes him under his wing.

October 1955

Each day, after school, sixteen-year-old Mozasu goes to help his mother at the market. One day he sees a male customer proposition and grope a pretty young stall holder and punches the man in the face. When the customer calls the police, Mozasu realises he has put himself in real danger, as Koreans who get into trouble with the law are at risk of deportation. As a police officer questions Mozasu and Sunja about the incident, Goro (the local pachinko parlour owner) intervenes. After Goro speaks up for Mozasu's good character, the police officer lets him off with a warning. Desperate to keep her son out of trouble, Sunja asks Goro if Mozasu can work for him. The pachinko parlour owner immediately agrees. He tells Mozasu to quit school the next day and then report to his shop.

March 1956

Mozasu is in his element working at the pachinko parlour. He aims to make enough money to buy a shop for his mother and pay for Noa's education. After six months, Goro announces that he wants Mozasu to be his foreman and takes him for a suit fitting. The seamstress they consult turns out to be the mother of his old friend, Haruki.

1957

Noa passes the entrance exam for Waseda University but his family have no way of paying his fees. Although Hansu has offered to fund all of Noa's expenses, Yoseb remains adamant that they should not accept money from him.

Hansu asks Noa to visit him at his office with Sunja. When they arrive, he congratulates Noa on his place at university and insists on taking them out for a celebratory meal. Desperate to secure her son's future, Sunja asks Hansu if he would loan them the money to pay the university fees. Hansu tells her that there is no need, as he has already paid Noa's tuition and board fees and has found him university accommodation. In private, Sunja tells Hansu that she wants to pay her son's fees herself and will reimburse him. Hansu, however, insists that he wants to help his son and threatens to tell Noa who he really is if Sunja refuses the gesture. Sunja reluctantly agrees to accept Hansu's assistance.

December 1959

Kim Changho decides to return to Korea, hoping that he can help reunify the divided country after the civil war. Concerned about who will take care of his wife when he dies, Yoseb tries to persuade Kim Changho to stay in Japan and eventually marry Kyunghee.

Kim Changho tells Kyunghee about her husband's proposition and suggests they could start a new life in Korea. Kyunghee refuses to consider the idea while her husband is still alive. Devastated, Kim Changho leaves in the middle of the night without saying goodbye.

Tokyo, 1960

Noa has been a student at Waseda University for two years and loves the scholarly life. He falls in love with Akiko—a beautiful Japanese student with radical ideas.

Osaka, April 1960

Twenty-year-old Mozasu is promoted by Goro from foreman to manager of one of the pachinko parlours. At Goro's insistence, they go to see Haruki's mother to have Mozasu measured for another new suit. Here Mozasu's eye is caught by Yumi—a new seamstress. Mozasu asks Yumi out to dinner but she refuses. As his jacket is being fitted, Mozasu deliberately rips the seams, giving him a reason to return the next day.

October 1961

Mozasu and Yumi have been dating for over a year and regularly attend an English evening class together. Mozasu plans to marry Yumi, although she wishes to live in America while he hopes to open his own pachinko parlour and eventually move back to Korea.

While waiting for Yumi outside her workplace, Mozasu is reunited with his old school friend, Haruki. Haruki is now a police officer and has avoided Mozasu as he has always been secretly in love with him.

Tokyo, March 1962

Noa meets Hansu once a month for lunch and Akiko becomes curious about her boyfriend's benefactor. When Hansu refuses to let her accompany him to lunch, Akiko appears at the restaurant uninvited and Hansu invites her to join them.

Once lunch is over and Hansu has gone, Noa expresses his fury at Akiko's disregard for his wishes. He tells her the relationship is over. Akiko accuses Noa of lying about Hansu saying that it is clear from their physical resemblance that Hansu is Noa's father. She also declares that it is obvious from Hansu's conspicuous wealth that he is a *yakuza* (gangster).

Noa goes back to Osaka and confronts Sunja who admits that Hansu is his father. Noa accuses her of ruining his life, claiming that he will never escape the taint of his father's blood.

Osaka, April 1962

Sunja receives a letter from Noa saying that he has withdrawn from university and moved to a new city to find a job. He asks her not to look for him and asserts that he wants nothing to do with his biological father.

Sunja goes to Hansu's house and is greeted by his wife, Mieko who assumes that Sunja is a beggar. Speaking to a Korean garden boy, Sunja explains that she is looking for her son and his master might know where Noa is. The boy tells her that Hansu is rarely at home but promises to relay the message when his master returns.

BOOK 3 — Pachinko — 1962-1989

Nagano, April 1962

After leaving Waseda University, Noa travels to Nagano. Sitting in a café by the train station he gets into conversation with the owner, Bingo. When Bingo learns that Noa is looking for work he says that there are always vacancies at Cosmos Pachinko. The local pachinko parlour is managed by one of his regular customers: Hideo Takano. Assuming that Noa is Japanese, Bingo mentions that Takano does not hire Koreans.

Noa goes to see Takano, introducing himself by his Japanese name—Nobuo Ban. The pachinko parlour manager offers him a bookkeeping job. When Takano asks, Noa swears that he is not Korean.

Osaka, April 1965

After two miscarriages, Yumi is pregnant for a third time. When his wife starts experiencing pains, Mozasu takes her to see a maternity specialist. Diagnosing high blood pressure, the doctor insists that Yumi must give up work and rest until she has the baby. To help her son and daughter-in-law, Sunja moves in with them to cook and clean. Thrown together, the women grow close. Yumi reveals that she was the child of a prostitute and a violent pimp and ran away from home with her younger sister when she was fourteen. At the end of her pregnancy, Yumi gives birth to a healthy baby boy named Solomon.

Yokohama, November 1968

Now the owner of his own pachinko parlour, Mozasu has moved his family to a large house in Yokohama. One day, at work, he receives a visit from the police who tell him that his wife and son have been hit by a drunk driver. Solomon escaped with minor injuries but Yumi died as she pushed her son to safety.

At Yumi's funeral, Mozasu sees Hansu for the first time in years. Mozasu tells Hansu that Sunja has been trying to get in touch with him regarding Noa's whereabouts. Their conversation is interrupted by Hansu's driver who says that a young woman urgently needs to talk to his boss. Hansu is furious when the young woman turns out to be Noriko—a hostess he has hired from a bar and left in the car during the funeral. Bored of waiting, she tells Hansu that she wants to go shopping. Hidden from the view of passers-by in the car, Hansu repeatedly hits Noriko until her face is covered in blood and she can no longer move. He instructs his driver to take him back to the office and then return Noriko to the hostess bar.

Sunja continues to live with Mozasu and takes care of Solomon. One day she finds Hansu waiting for her outside Solomon's school. She refuses to speak to him until he tells her he is dying of prostate cancer. Oblivious to his grandmother's discomfort, Solomon invites Hansu to have dinner with them. At the house, Hansu meets Haruki who is a regular dinner guest. Having collected information on all of Sunja's associates, he knows that the detective is homosexual but is engaged to a woman called Ayame.

Nagano, January 1969

After working for Cosmos Pachinko for seven years, Noa has been promoted to head of the business offices. Although still evading contact with his parents, he sends money to his mother every month and has paid back his debt to Hansu.

Noa begins dating Risa—a filing clerk in the offices. Although Japanese and from a middle-class family, Risa is tainted by the disgrace of her father: a doctor who accidentally killed two of his patients and then killed himself. Noa and Risa marry and have twin girls, then a boy and another girl in quick succession. Although feeling affection for his wife, Noa does not love her with the same passion that he felt for Akiko. Still posing as Japanese, even to his wife and children, he continually lives in fear of discovery.

Yokohama, July 1974

Giving in to pressure from his mother, Haruki marries Ayame who takes over the dressmaking business as well as caring for Haruki's younger brother, Daisuke. When Haruki's mother dies Ayame decides to sell the dressmaking shop. They move to Yokohama, using Hansu's connections in high places to secure Haruki a transfer.

Ayame devotes herself to caring for her husband's younger brother who needs around the clock care. Although now thirty, Daisuke still has the mental age of a young child. Ayame's only respite is when a special education teacher comes to visit Daisuke. Then she goes shopping and to the public baths. One day, on the way home from the baths, she walks through the park and sees two men engaged in a sexual act. She flees the scene but then returns to see further couples having sex (an intimacy that she and her husband no longer engage in).

Three days later Ayame returns to the park and is approached by a beautiful girl. The girl promises to do pleasurable things with Ayame if she returns with money. After avoiding the park for three months Ayame returns. Once again, there are many couples engaged in sexual activity. Watching two men making love, Ayame realises that one of them is her husband. After Haruki and his partner leave, Ayame is approached by the girl she met on her previous visit. Tempted by her offers of love, she is about to

27

succumb when the girl starts searching through Ayame's bag for money. Disgusted, Ayame pushes her away. She returns home and says nothing to Haruki about what she witnessed.

Yokohama, March 1976

Haruki interviews the parents of a twelve-year-old Korean boy who committed suicide by jumping off the roof of an apartment building. The father shows Haruki his son's middle school graduation album. Across the flyleaf are racist insults written by his son's Japanese classmates—one of which suggests that he should kill himself. Haruki sadly tells the parents that nothing can be done to punish the children who bullied their son.

Haunted by the boy's suicide, Haruki meets Mozasu for dinner and admits that he has wanted to kill himself many times since he was a child. Mozasu reveals that his classmates wrote similar things in his own graduation book and that he also wanted to die when he was at school. He suffered a similar sense of hopelessness after Yumi died but carried on for Solomon's sake. Now his life looks brighter again as he has found love with a Japanese restaurant owner—Etsuko.

Nagano, August 1978

Hansu contacts Sunja to tell her that he has traced Noa to Nagano. He reveals that their son runs a pachinko parlour, goes by his Japanese name and even his wife and children do not know that he is Korean.

Hansu advises Sunja against approaching her son, suggesting that they should respect the fact that he does not want to see them. He drives her to Noa's workplace so she can covertly catch a glimpse of him. As soon as Sunja sees Noa outside his offices, she cannot control the urge to rush over to him. Noa briefly speaks to his mother but claims urgent business and promises to call her that evening. Later, Sunja realises that Noa does not have her number in Yokohama. The next morning Hansu calls with the news that Noa shot himself only moments after she had spoken to him.

Yokohama, 1979

Mozasu's Japanese girlfriend, Etsuko, is a divorcee who relinquished custody of her three children after committing adultery. As the disgrace of Etsuko's behaviour made her children social outcasts, she has a troubled relationship with her fifteen-year-old daughter and her adult sons refuse all contact. Mozasu is eager to marry Etsuko but she refuses as her mother insists that marrying a Korean pachinko parlour owner will heap further shame on her children.

On Solomon's fourteenth birthday, Mozasu and Etsuko have to take him to apply for his alien registration card. In Japan, this is a legal requirement for all Koreans born after 1952 and the card must be renewed every three years.

Earlier in the day, Etsuko received a call from her daughter, Hana. Announcing that she was pregnant, Hana informed her mother that she was coming to stay with her. Hana arrives in Yokohama just in time for Solomon's lavish birthday party.

Osaka, 1979

Sunja returns to Osaka and discovers that her mother has stomach cancer. Yoseb has died and Kyunghee has been nursing Yangjin. In her final days, Yangjin shocks Kyunghee and Sunja by speaking her mind. She dwells on the shame that Sunja brought on her family when she fell pregnant by Hansu and tells Kyunghee that she should have married Kim Changho.

Meanwhile, in Yokohama, Hana has a termination and continues to stay in her mother's apartment. Bored, she devotes herself to seducing Solomon.

At Yangjin's funeral, Hansu tells Sunja that his wife has died and that he wants her to marry him. Sunja refuses, suddenly furious that Hansu has outlived both her mother and her son.

Yokohama, 1980

After losing his virginity to Hana, Solomon becomes infatuated with her. Most days, they meet in secret at Etsuko's apartment and make love. Soon, Hana begins asking Solomon for money and he happily obliges. When Solomon's money runs out, Hana leaves

29

Yokohama without warning.

New York, 1985

At college in New York, Solomon receives a call from Hana. After leaving her mother's apartments Hana has worked as a hostess in Tokyo but refuses to reveal her address to her family. Solomon persuades Hana to give him her number but when he tries to call her back he gets through to a Chinese restaurant.

Months later, Etsuko discovers from a private investigator that Hana is working in a Turkish bath. She waits for her daughter outside her workplace and is shocked at her ravaged appearance.

Tokyo, 1989

After graduating from college, Solomon returns to Japan with his Korean-American girlfriend Phoebe. Phoebe is unhappy in Tokyo as she is not eligible for a work visa and speaks little Japanese. Born in the United States, she is taken aback by racist attitudes towards Koreans in Japan.

Solomon works for Travis Brothers—a British-owned investment bank. One day, when Solomon is winning at poker, one of his colleagues refers to the fact that Solomon's father is a rich pachinko parlour owner. Disconcerted, Solomon deliberately loses the hand.

Solomon's boss, Kazu, is Japanese but was educated in the United States. Realising that Solomon lost the poker game deliberately, Kazu advises him to ignore his colleague's casual racism. He also expresses outrage at the way his nation has treated the Korean people. Shortly afterwards Kazu asks Solomon to join an elite team who are working on an important real estate deal. Travis Brothers are trying to purchase land for a client who wishes to build a golf course in Yokohama. The deal involves persuading three landowners to sell up but one of them—an old lady named Sonoko Matsuda—is proving immune to financial incentives.

Yokohama, 1989

Solomon takes Phoebe to Yokohama to visit his family. He tells his father about the real estate deal and asks if he knows anything about the old lady who is holding up the project. Mozasu promises to consult Goro.

The next day Mozasu calls Solomon and tells him that Sonoko Matsuda is a Korean and does not want to sell her property to the Japanese. She is, however, prepared to sell to Goro. Goro has offered to buy the property from her and will then sell on to the bank's Japanese client. Solomon breaks the news to Kazu who is delighted.

Tokyo, 1989

Hana is dying of AIDS and Solomon visits her in hospital. He urges her to go to the USA where there are more advanced medications, but Hana tells him she does not want to live.

When Solomon returns to the office, Kazu tells him that Sonoko Matsuda died only days after Goro sold her property to their client. The client has now cancelled the sale, claiming that the timing of the old lady's death looks suspicious. Kazu tells Solomon that the bank cannot afford to be associated with *yakuza* and will have to let Solomon go. Solomon realises that Kazu chose him for the project to exploit his Korean connections. After being escorted from the building, he asks a taxi driver to take him to Yokohama.

Solomon seeks out his father who is in a café with Goro and Haruki. Goro assures Solomon that ninety-three-year-old Sonoko died of a heart attack and that Kazu has simply used her death as an excuse to fire him.

Solomon returns to Tokyo and again visits Hana in hospital. Hana suggests that Solomon should take over his father's pachinko business.

When Phoebe learns that Solomon has been fired, she immediately suggests that they return to the United States. If they marry, Solomon would be granted citizenship. Solomon, however, does not want to marry Phoebe as he dislikes her anti-Japanese attitude. He also realises that he does not want to be an American, even though this would make Phoebe and his father happy.

Phoebe returns to the United States alone and Solomon goes to Yokohama to see his father. Mozasu is upset when Solomon tells him he wants to be involved with the pachinko business. Having paid for his son to attend American schools, he hoped that his son would escape prejudice by getting a respectable job.

31

Seventy-three-year-old Sunja visits Isak's grave and cries as she thinks about Noa. The groundskeeper approaches her, revealing that he knows Sunja has two sons and a grandson because he has seen them all visit the grave. He observes that, while Mozasu still visits every month, he has not seen Noa for eleven years. Sunja is astonished to learn that Noa regularly visited Isak's grave even when he was in hiding. She buries a photo key ring with pictures of Noa and Mozasu by Isak's tombstone.

GLOSSARY

Min Jin Lee immerses readers in the culture of her characters by using Korean and Japanese words and phrases without providing an English translation. Often the rough meaning of these words is apparent by their context. Occasionally, their meaning is less obvious. Below is a glossary of Korean/Japanese words in their order of appearance in the novel.

BOOK 1

Chapter 2

Ajumoni — Yangjin is addressed this way by her lodgers and servants. It literally means aunt and is a formal way to address a married woman.
Hanbok — a traditional Korean dress
Baek Isak — Like Western names, Korean names have two parts: a family name and a given name. In Korean names, the family name (In Isak's case, Baek) traditionally comes before the first.

Chapter 3

Yangban — an upper-class Korean
Uh-muh — Oh dear! /Oh, my goodness!

Chapter 5

Oppa — means older brother but may be used by a younger woman when talking to an older man

Chapter 7

Jesa — a Korean ceremony commemorating the ancestors of the participants

Chapter 8

Chima — a traditional Korean skirt that ties just above the chest

Chapter 9

Udon — noodles

Chapter 10

Ajeossi — greeting used to address a middle-aged elder male
Waaaaah — Wow!

Chapter 11

Yobo — a term of endearment (often used between husband and wife)
Abuji — father
Omoni — mother

Chapter 12

six-mat house — In Japan the size of a house or room is conveyed by the number of tatami mats that would cover its floorspace. The measurements of tatami mats can vary but one mat generally covers about 1.5 square metres.

Chapter 13

Arirang — a well-known Korean folk song often considered to be the unofficial national anthem of Korea

Chapter 14

Shotengai — A Japanese shopping district

Aigoo — an expression of frustration
Onsen — a Japanese spa

Chapter 15

Kimchi — a Korean dish of spicy pickled cabbage
Tsumei — adopted Japanese name
Daikon — a winter radish
Sento — Japanese communal baths
Hanko — a personal seal or stamp
Genmaicha — green tea combined with roasted brown rice

Chapter 17

Doburoku — an alcoholic drink similar to sake

BOOK 2

Chapter 1

Shinto — the traditional religion of Japan

Chapter 2

Gochujang — red chili pepper paste
Doenjang — soybean paste
Bento — a wooden Japanese lunchbox
Oishi! — delicious!
Agasshi — young lady
Banchan — Korean side dishes
Yakiniku — grilled meat
Galbi — grilled ribs
Buta — pig
Korokke — croquettes
Yakisoba — A noodle stir fry dish

Chapter 4

Aga — little one/child

Chapter 10

Burakumin — an outcast group at the bottom of Japanese society. As such, they were the subject of extreme discrimination and ostracism

Chapter 11

Taiyaki — a Japanese fish-shaped cake
Gimbap — a popular Korean takeout snack
Iyada — an expression of non-agreement
Yakitori — skewered chicken
Maji — an expression of surprise similar to Really? /Seriously?
Hai — yes
Kanji — a system of Japanese writing using Chinese characters

Chapter 15

Soo nee — yeah, sure!

Chapter 16

Honto desu — it's true

Chapter 17

Noonchi — the ability to gauge social situations and act accordingly

Chapter 18

Sushi-ya — sushi restaurant
Hanja — the Korean name for Chinese written characters
Obi — a sash worn around the waist of a kimono

Chapter 20

Umeboshi — pickled *ume* fruits (*ume* are similar to plums)

BOOK 3

Chapter 3

Toruko — Turkish baths

Chapter 4

Kaiju — monster
Hajimemashite — pleased to meet you

Chapter 5

Mizu shobai — The Japanese night-time entertainment industry (hostess bars etc.)
Sumimasen — excuse me

Chapter 6

Cha — tea
Senbei — Japanese rice crackers

Chapter 7

Combini — convenience store
Mindan — a pro-South Korean organisation in Japan
Chosenjin — a pro-North Korean organisation in Japan
Sho ga nai — nothing can be done about it
Izakaya — a type of Japanese bar

Chapter 9

Nani — What?
Unmei — destiny
Yukata — a light kimono
Arigato — Thanks a lot

Chapter 10

Moshi-moshi — Hello (when answering the telephone)

Chapter 11

Iie — No

Chapter 12

Boushi — hat

Chapter 13

Halmoni — grandma
Unagiya — eel restaurant

Chapter 16

Gomen nasai — I am sorry
Hapa — a person of mixed ethnic origin
Sensei — teacher (in martial arts)

Chapter 18

Pajeon — a traditional Korean pancake

Chapter 19

Tsugoi — Wow! / Amazing!
Hatsukoi — first love

Chapter 20

Irasshai — welcome
Gaijin — foreigner
Otomodachi — great friend

STYLE

Min Jin Lee's multigenerational story is incredibly ambitious in its scope. Covering seven decades (from 1910–1989), it introduces a huge cast of characters and encompasses history, race, politics and gender. Like Noa in *Pachinko*, Lee is an admirer of the nineteenth-century English novel. This taste for the classics is reflected in her writing style. Although she uses language in a typically modern, pared back way, the sprawling spectrum of *Pachinko* is reminiscent of the novels of Charles Dickens: a writer who was never afraid to dazzle readers with a dizzying range of characters, sub-plots and themes. Lee's interest in the struggles of ordinary men and women in a largely unjust society is also a recurring theme in Dickens's fiction. While Dickens generally provided happy endings for his protagonists, however, the destinies of Lee's characters often have more in common with Thomas Hardy's tragic literary creations who strive but fail to overcome life's adversities.

Fans of *Great Expectations* may spot a striking similarity between Noa's story and that of Pip in Dickens's novel. Pip comes from humble origins but becomes a gentleman thanks to a benefactor who pays for his education. Having always assumed that his patron is Miss Havisham (the guardian of the woman he loves), he is horrified to discover that it is Abel Magwitch (an escaped convict) who has bankrolled his lifestyle. In *Pachinko*, this moment is echoed when Noa realises not only that Hansu is his father but also that much of the money that has funded his education has been made through criminal activities. Both characters feel their futures are tainted by the discovery.

Lee takes on a further common feature of nineteenth-century fiction by choosing to use an omniscient narrator in her novel—an increasingly rare phenomenon in contemporary fiction. By employing a God-like narrator who has an overview of all the characters' actions and thoughts, Lee is able to tell the story of a whole community. Democratically conveying the perspectives of all characters—even the minor ones—she gives a multitude of voices to people who have largely been forgotten by history.

Min Jin Lee has stated that one of her main aims as a writer is to create "radical empathy through art". By conveying the humanity of each and every one of her Korean characters, Lee hopes to redress mankind's tendency to "dehumanize entire populations". This seems a particularly important goal at a time when Western perceptions of Koreans may be based solely upon news coverage of the North Korean leader, Kim Jong-un. As Lee points out, "it makes it very easy to bomb North Korea if we pretend they're all one person. Literature makes it harder to dehumanize people in this way."

CHARACTERS

There are over forty named characters in *Pachinko* spanning several generations. The following lists the most significant ones in rough order of appearance.

SOUTH KOREA

Hoonie Kim

Hoonie is the character who begins the multi-generational story of *Pachinko*. The only surviving child of his parents, he is born with a cleft palate and a twisted foot—afflictions that are interpreted by others as a curse. Nevertheless, Hoonie's thoughtful nature means that he is respected by all who know him.

Hoonie is kind and considerate to his young wife, Yangjin, and dotes on their only surviving child, Sunja. He dies from tuberculosis.

Hoonie's Parents

The spirit of resilience that runs through Lee's novel begins with Hoonie's parents. When Korea is annexed by Japan and rents are raised by the colonial government, they respond by sleeping in the anteroom of the kitchen in order to rent their bedroom to lodgers.

Due to their son's disability, Hoonie's ageing parents worry about his future. They ensure they provide him with the best chances in life by raising him to be skilled and self-sufficient. When the unexpected opportunity arises to buy him a bride, Hoonie's mother snaps up the offer, keen to secure her son's happiness.

Yangjin

Yangjin is fifteen years old when she marries Hoonie and first meets him on their wedding day. Nevertheless, she grows to love her kind and gentle husband.

When Hoonie dies, Yangjin is devastated but shows her inner strength when she returns to work the day after his burial. Knowing that she must fend for herself and her child, she works hard to make sure the boarding house always has a full complement of lodgers.

Yangjin shoulders another great loss when her daughter leaves for Japan after marrying Isak. Although it is likely that she will never see Sunja again, she makes the painful sacrifice willingly as she knows that her daughter and grandchild will face disgrace if they remain in Korea. Her practicality again comes to the fore when she gives Sunja two gold rings to sell in case of emergency.

Yangjin disappears from the story for eleven years until, as a favour to Sunja, Hansu brings her to Japan from Korea. Her malnourished state speaks volumes about the hardships suffered by Korean citizens in those intervening years. When Hansu finds her, she has lost the boarding house due to raised taxes. Working as a housekeeper for a Japanese merchant, she has been sleeping in a storeroom.

In her final days, before she dies of stomach cancer, Yangjin feels a kind of liberation. Having spent her entire life toiling, she submits to being tended to by Sunja and Kyunghee, knowing there is nothing left for her to do. She also undergoes something of a metamorphosis in personality, shocking her daughter and Kyunghee by speaking her mind about issues on which she has previously remained silent. Accusing Sunja of being a poor daughter, she criticises her for falling pregnant by Hansu. She also pronounces that Kyunghee made a mistake when she rejected Kim Changho.

Yangjin's Father

Yangjin's father is a victim of Japan's colonisation of Korea. A tenant farmer, he loses his lease as a result of the government's new land surveys. Unable to afford to keep his four daughters, he marries them off.

Sunja

While certain characters come and go in the novel, Sunja is central to the story. The plot of *Pachinko* really gets going when she falls pregnant—an event which will instigate the family's migration to Japan. The novel also ends with her reflections as a 73-year-old grandmother.

Like her father, Sunja is an adored only child but is born with seemingly limited prospects. Although she does not inherit either of Hoonie's physical disabilities, her marriage prospects are harmed by the possibility that she may carry defective genes.

Much of Sunja's charm as a character springs from her down-to-earth nature. Hard-working and pragmatic, she rolls up her sleeves and gets on with life with minimum fuss. Although not conventionally beautiful, there is a grace in her strength and straightforwardness which attracts others— including the wealthy fish broker, Koh Hansu.

Sixteen-year-old Sunja shows her youthful naivety when she falls in love with Hansu, never considering that he might already be married. Drawn to his air of sophistication, she loves to hear his stories about Osaka—a place that sounds incredibly glamorous to her. Little does she know that her relationship with Hansu will lead her to live in Osaka, but the city will not prove as enticing as she anticipated.

When Sunja falls pregnant by Hansu and discovers that he has a wife in Japan, she is heartbroken and ashamed. Hansu, however, does not see a problem, happily offering to set her up in a comfortable home where he can visit her as his "Korean wife". Given Sunja's limited options at this point, it is a sign of her moral integrity and independence of spirit that she refuses. Without hesitation, she renounces the man she loves and his financial assistance, choosing to go it alone. This decision sets into motion a chain of events where she will have less and less agency over her life. To escape social disgrace, she will marry Isak and travel to Japan where her life as a migrant will be unrelentingly tough.

Despite the hardships of life in Japan, Sunja retains her resilient and resourceful spirit. When her brother-in-law gets into trouble with a moneylender, she pays off his debt by selling a watch Hansu gave her, squeezing a good price from a wily pawnbroker. Similarly, when Isak goes to prison, she supports her children by selling *kimchi* in the intimidating atmosphere of the local market. Sunja's tireless work ethic and determination reflect the actions of many first-generation Korean women in Japan who did whatever was necessary to keep their families alive—from working in markets selling homemade goods to raising livestock inside their homes.

As her sons grow older, Sunja experiences a conflict between her independent spirit and her love for her children. Unable to cover Noa's university expenses, she reluctantly accepts Hansu's assistance—a decision which involves swallowing her pride and compromising her moral integrity. Although she takes this step to secure her son's future happiness, it has tragic results. Noa discovers that Hansu is his father, breaks off contact with his family, and eventually kills himself, leaving Sunja haunted by the idea that, if she had made different choices, her son would still be alive.

After Noa's death, Sunja loses much of her spirit, although she continues to make herself useful to her family, looking after her grandson, Solomon, when his mother dies. Nevertheless, when she looks back on her life, she reflects that "Beyond the dailiness, there had been moments of shimmering beauty and some glory, too". While she has suffered intensely, she refuses to let this eclipse the joys of her life—her marriage to Isak, and the birth of her sons.

Isak

When Isak arrives at Yangjin's boarding house, he immediately stands out from the average lodger. Handsome and elegantly dressed, he is a gentleman and a scholar. Born into a wealthy family in North Korea, Isak has spent his time immersed in books and sheltered from the world due to his frail constitution. Seeking to make a positive contribution to society, he is on his way to Osaka in Japan where he will take up the role of Associate Pastor of a Presbyterian church.

On arriving at the boarding house, Isak falls seriously ill with tuberculosis and the women of the house nurse him back to health. Learning that Sunja is to have a fatherless child, he sees an opportunity to repay the family's kindness. While he has previously held back from marriage (aware that any wife might soon become a widow), he feels that marrying Sunja can only improve her situation.

Isak proves to be a man as kind and considerate as Sunja's father. Completely selfless, he values the happiness of his family above his own. Despite only fathering Mozasu, he loves his sons equally and earns Sunja's affection without ever making her feel beholden to him.

Isak's innocence and gentle nature make him an extremely endearing character but are also shown to be impractical qualities in an often cruel and hostile world. When Isak arrives in Japan, his naivety is highlighted when he discovers his salary will not be enough to live on. Previously sheltered from financial issues, he also fails to think about how his brother Yoseb raised the money to pay for his passage to Japan. He only realises that Yoseb borrowed the substantial sum when debt collectors come knocking on the door.

Isak's naivety ends up leading, indirectly, to his death. When his colleague, Sexton Hu, takes a stand against the Japanese repression of Christianity (by mouthing the Lord's Prayer before a Shinto shrine), Isak admires the young man's courage. He does not foresee that Sexton Hu's protest will lead them all to be arrested and imprisoned. His fate reflects the Japanese government's mistrust of Presbyterian pastors who led the Korean independence movement.

Isak is finally released to die at home after two years—a common policy to avoid the inconvenience of Korean prisoners dying in jail. In his final days, he demonstrates that his mistreatment in prison has not dimmed his spirituality or goodness. He dies without bitterness, happy to be reunited with his wife and sons.

Koh Hansu

At thirty-four years old, Koh Hansu is more than twice Sunja's age when they first meet. Nevertheless, the wealthy fish broker stands out like a movie star with his immaculate Western suits and perfect command of Japanese.

Hansu is, in fact, a native of Jeju in South Korea who has risen from lowly origins. Moving to Osaka with his drunken father when he was twelve, young Hansu ensured they survived "through foraging, hunting, and petty theft.". What he initially fails to tell Sunja is that he shares his mansion in Osaka with his wife (the daughter of a powerful Japanese moneylender) and three daughters.

Hansu's immediate attraction to Sunja reveals something of his complex nature. While the age gap smacks of a man trying to recapture his youth, his choice of Sunja, in particular, is significant. Hansu is drawn to intelligent, hard-working women and Sunja's manner and sturdy physique reflect both these qualities. Meanwhile, her complete lack of flirtatious guile indicates straightforwardness and innocence.

Sunja resists Hansu's attempts at conversation until he rescues her from a group of Japanese schoolboys who are threatening to rape her. This encounter neatly illustrates the two sides of Hansu's personality. While showing kindly concern and protectiveness towards Sunja, he makes sinister death threats to the boys. Sunja, meanwhile, remains oblivious to the nature of Hansu's dark threats as she does not understand Japanese.

Hansu does not immediately attempt to seduce Sunja, courting her for three months before the relationship is consummated. It is left for readers to decide if this shows respect for Sunja or whether it illustrates a calculated grooming process. Certainly, at the beginning of their relationship, he disingenuously invites Sunja to think of him as an older brother and friend when he clearly has a completely different relationship in mind.

Hansu's disregard for conventional morality is demonstrated when Sunja tells him that she is pregnant. After revealing that he already has a wife and daughters, Hansu is excited at the prospect of having a son with Sunja. Having kept many mistresses during his marriage, he sees no reason why Sunja cannot be his second "wife". He is, therefore, confused when Sunja reacts with distress and horror to his revelation and rejects his offer to house and keep her.

When, years later, Hansu traces Sunja in Japan, he engineers a plan to ensure that she has enough money. Realising that she will not accept assistance from him, he uses Kim Changho as a front to offer her a job in his restaurant. Hansu only reveals that he was behind this piece of good fortune when he feels the need to intervene again—this time when he foresees that Japan will lose the war and Osaka will be bombed. After convincing Sunja to leave Osaka for Tamaguchi's farm, Hansu takes the opportunity to get to know Noa and makes it clear that he wishes to be part of his son's life.

Sunja succeeds in keeping Hansu at arm's length until the time comes for Noa to go to university. Aware that Sunja will not be able to afford his university fees, Hansu pays them all in advance. In doing so, he succeeds in buying his way into Noa's life. Again, this illustrates Hansu's opportunist nature, but the gesture also springs from a genuine desire to help Noa become a scholar. A self-educated man, with no formal qualifications, Hansu admires scholarly men and is delighted at the prospect of his son joining their ranks. Unable to be a father to Noa, he settles for being his benefactor and, to his credit, never reveals his true identity to his son.

Although Hansu's dealings with Sunja and Noa show that he is capable of caring for others, this is shown to be within a limited sphere. The protectiveness he feels for Sunja and Noa does not extend, for example, to Sunja's in-laws. This is demonstrated when he cunningly removes Yoseb from the picture after learning that he may prevent Sunja from leaving Osaka for the safety of Tamaguchi's farm. By arranging a well-paid job for Yoseb in Nagasaki, Hansu silences any potential objections. This leaves readers to wonder whether he realises he is resigning Sunja's brother-in-law to a terrible fate. Although Hansu could not know with certainty that Nagasaki would be bombed, given his accurate prediction about Osaka, it is likely he knew it to be a strong possibility. He shows a similarly ruthless streak when he lies to Yoseb and Kyunghee, claiming that their parents have died in Korea. Hansu does not know this to be a fact but makes the claim to discourage the entire family from returning to Korea.

While it may be argued that Hansu's retrieval of Yangjin from South Korea shows compassion, even this is not as generous an act as it first seems. Although he has had the means to trace Yangjin before, Hansu only takes action when Sunja specifically asks him to find out if she is safe. Seeing an opportunity to be the recipient of Sunja's gratitude, he springs into action.

An individualist, Hansu believes that "thinking about the group" is a serious flaw in Japanese and Korean society. Lacking any sense of duty to Korea, Japan, or society as a whole, he is uninterested in politics or in who wins the war—only how the outcome will affect him personally. Underlying this attitude is a deep cynicism about human nature, illustrated when he declares, "People are rotten everywhere you go." His way of looking at life forms a stark contrast to Isak's selflessness, idealism and desire to make a positive contribution to society.

As the novel progresses, we gain a clearer idea of just how corrupt Hansu's line of work is as we see him involved in the black market and operating a protection racket. We also glimpse his violent side in the scene after Yumi's funeral. After politely offering his condolences to the family, he returns to his car and beats a young hostess senseless for having the temerity to send the driver to interrupt him. This shocking incident illustrates the contradictions in Hansu's character. Hiring the hostess as he wishes to be seen with a beautiful young woman, he is then infuriated by her lack of intelligence. His reaction reflects the fact that he still desires Sunja. Significantly, Hansu's driver watches the assault, too frightened to intervene. Aware of a former employee of Hansu's who lost part of his finger for failing to line up shoes properly, he is in no hurry to suffer the same fate.

Bokhee & Dokhee

Bokhee and Dokhee are orphaned sisters employed by Yangjin as servant girls in her boarding house. When Yangjin has to give up the lodging house, they are approached by a woman from Seoul who offers them factory jobs in Manchuria. Excited, the girls promise Yangjin that they will return when they have made enough money to buy the boarding house. As Yangjin never hears from the girls again, it is likely that they suffer the fate that Hansu warns Sunja about. Lured away by the promise of good jobs, young Korean women were forced into prostitution to service Japanese soldiers.

The Chung Brothers

The Chung brothers are three fishermen who lodge with Yangjin. Despite sleeping with other lodgers crammed into one room, they feel grateful for their accommodation, which is better than most. The skinny physique of the youngest brother, Fatso, belies his enormous appetite.

Jun

Jun is the talkative coalman who supplies Yangjin's boarding house.

Jun's Wife

A hardworking woman, Jun's wife sells seaweed at the market in Busan, South Korea. She is also fond of making declarations about a woman's lot. Before Sunja meets Koh Hansu, Jun's wife declares "a woman's life is endless work and suffering." She also claims, "For a woman, the man you marry will determine the quality of your life completely." Both statements prove to have some truth in them.

Pastor Shin

Isak visits the pastor of the church in Busan to talk over his plan to marry Sunja. Pastor Shin clearly does not share Isak's selfless nature as he is incredulous that he would be prepared to make such a sacrifice. Before he marries the couple, he subjects Sunja to severe questioning, as he wishes to protect Isak. Shin has, however, known great suffering himself, having lost his wife and four children to cholera.

Through Pastor Shin, we first learn about the antireligious policies of the Korean colonial government when he tells Isak that his congregation are afraid to attend his services. This foreshadows the religious persecution Isak will become a victim of in Japan.

JAPAN

Yoseb

Yoseb is as different from his younger brother, Isak, as it is possible to be. As a child, he disliked school and did not feel the faith in God that motivated the rest of his family. Leaving Korea as a young man, he sought a new life in Japan, working his way up from machinist to the foreman of a biscuit factory in Osaka. It is he who encourages his younger brother to move to Japan.

Yoseb and his wife, Kyunghee, are both from wealthy Korean families but live in greatly reduced circumstances in Japan. Despite Yoseb's good job, they live in little more than a shack in the

Korean ghetto as Koreans are paid much less than Japanese workers. Nevertheless, Yoseb is extremely generous to Isak, instinctively wanting to protect him. Without telling his brother, he borrows money to pay for his passage to Japan. He also refuses to accept any contribution to the household expenses.

Privately, Yoseb worries about "how to take care of his family in this strange and difficult land." Masculine pride leads him to bear this burden alone, as he believes in upholding traditional Korean gender roles (where the husband is the sole breadwinner while the wife keeps house). Refusing to allow Kyunghee to work (despite her desire to do so), he secretly repairs machines at night to make extra money, scrubbing his hands to hide the tell-tale signs of his second job.

Yoseb is furious when he discovers that Sunja has paid off his loan and Kyunghee accompanied her to the pawnbroker. In his eyes, their behaviour undermines his authority as head of the household. Eventually, however, he is forced to accept that, in Japan, he cannot afford the luxury of traditional ideals. Financial necessity means he allows Sunja and Kyunghee to start their pickle business and, later, to work in a restaurant. Backed into a corner he reflects, "Which was worse—his wife working for moneylenders or him owing money to them? For a Korean man, the choices were always shit."

When Isak is arrested, Yoseb is devastated, blaming himself for bringing his brother to Japan. After Isak dies, he is never the same again becoming cynical and withdrawn. His life then takes a further cruel downturn when he takes a job in Nagasaki (arranged by Hansu) and suffers horrific burns in the American atomic bombing of the city. Wracked with pain, he is dependent on expensive medications and his condition only worsens over the years. Unable to fulfil his main objective in life (to take care of his family) he feels it would be better if he were dead, as he would no longer be a burden.

Through suffering, Yoseb becomes a humbler man. Putting aside his own feelings, he makes a noble gesture of self-sacrifice. Aware that Kim Changho is in love with his wife, he asks him to stay in Japan and marry Kyunghee once he dies.

Kyunghee

When Sunja arrives in Japan, Yoseb's wife, Kyunghee, is immediately accepting of her sister-in-law—despite the unusual circumstances of Sunja's marriage to Isak. The two women go on to become close friends and a source of great support to each other.

Kyunghee is thirty-one when Sunja first meets her. After growing up in a wealthy household with servants, she has adjusted with grace to living in the squalor of a ghetto, ensuring the interior of her modest home is as clean and welcoming as possible. Despite desperately wanting a child, she has accepted the fact that she is infertile without bitterness. While a lesser woman might be jealous of Sunja's pregnancy, she views it as a blessing that will, at last, bring a child into her home.

Kyunghee never openly defies or complains about her husband's restrictive ideas about the role of women. Nevertheless, beneath her beautiful and acquiescent surface lies an astute and resourceful woman who does everything she can to improve her family's circumstances. It is her idea to buy their house rather than pay a landlord each month and she is thrifty enough to save money from Yoseb's meagre wages to send to their parents. Appreciating the advantages of speaking Japanese, she listens to the radio to improve her accent.

When Kyunghee reveals that she dreams of having her own *kimchi* business we see a conflict between her ambitions and a genuine desire not to go against her husband's wishes. Increasing financial hardship means that, eventually, Yoseb can no longer object to the scheme. Even so, Kyunghee is sensitive to her husband's views, refraining from selling at the market and initially refusing to go inside Kim Changho's restaurant.

Kyunghee grows lonely in her marriage as Yoseb becomes increasingly withdrawn—first when Isak dies and then when he suffers terrible burns in the bombing of Nagasaki. Through it all, Kyunghee remains loyal to her husband, despite knowing that Kim Changho is in love with her. Kyunghee cares for Kim Changho but, even when Yoseb gives his approval, she refuses to consider a relationship with him while her husband is still alive. Her selfless decision is also influenced by her belief that Kim Changho deserves to marry a woman who can give him children. The sacrifice causes Kyunghee a great deal of pain as she grieves his absence when he leaves for Korea.

Noa

From the day of his birth, the identity of Sunja's eldest child—Noa—is conflicted. Raised by Isak, and believing him to be his biological father, Noa is a carbon copy of Sunja's husband in many ways, sharing his quiet intelligence, gentlemanly mannerisms, love of books and idealism. Noa's true biological father has also left his stamp on him, however, as physically he looks just like Hansu.

Noa's divided sense of self becomes apparent when he starts attending school. Even as an eight-year-old, he is meticulous about his appearance, looking "like a middle-class Japanese child from a wealthier part of town". Unbeknown to his parents, he also chooses to go by his Japanese name, Nobuo Boku. Although at this stage in his life, pretending to be Japanese is not an option, he does all that he can to dissociate himself from his Korean identity, choosing solitude over mixing with other Korean children. Despite his efforts, Noa cannot shake off the burden of shame he feels at being Korean. His sense of being tainted is exacerbated when he is made to sit with the schoolchildren whose families keep pigs due to the strong smell of *kimchi* on his clothes.

When Isak is imprisoned, Noa loses his faith in God. Still, he does not lose sight of his idealistic aim of being a "good Korean". When he needs to earn money to fund his studies, he rejects the pachinko business in favour of a badly paid position as a bookkeeper, which he feels is more respectable. At university, he chooses to study English literature over subjects with greater earning potential. Despite the fact that public schools do not hire Koreans, he dreams of becoming an English teacher.

Noa's idealistic vision of his future comes crashing down when he discovers that Hansu is his father. The devastating discovery that he is not Isak's son is made worse by his realisation that Hansu is a *yakuza* and the money that has funded his education has come from organised crime. In the light of this new knowledge, Noa feels irredeemably contaminated by both the money he has accepted and the blood that runs through his veins.

In an act of self-flagellation, Noa cuts himself off from his family and leaves the scholarly life to work in pachinko—a business he has always despised. Choosing at random to live in Nagano, he begins to pass himself off as Japanese when he applies for a job as a pachinko parlour bookkeeper, knowing that the owner does not hire Koreans. Ironically, in trying to escape from his connection to Hansu (and pay back his debt to him), he becomes further enmeshed in a world that he has always considered dirty.

Noa goes on to become wealthy and successful and have a family of his own but is unable to enjoy any of these blessings. As even his wife and children believe him to be Japanese, he lives in continual fear of discovery. When Sunja eventually finds him, he feels a strange sense of relief, knowing that the pretence is over. Shooting himself only moments after his mother has gone, he demonstrates that he would rather die than be exposed as a Korean.

Eleven years after his death, Sunja makes the surprising discovery that Noa regularly visited his father's grave, even when he was in hiding. This revelation suggests that, despite appearing to turn on his back on all the ideals that he shared with Isak, Noa still considered him to be his true father.

Mozasu

Mozasu is the son of Sunja and Isak and six years younger than his brother, Noa. Although exactly like Isak in looks, his personality is nothing like that of his placid, idealistic father.

At school, Mozasu suffers the same taunts from Japanese children that his brother underwent—an experience which, years later, he admits led him to consider suicide. Nevertheless, his outward reaction to this persecution is completely different from that of his brother. Lacking Noa's academic abilities, Mozasu sees no point in trying to become a "good Korean" and responds with defiance, often getting into trouble for violent outbursts. Instead of aspiring to an education and a respectable profession, he dreams of becoming rich.

One of the greatest ironies of the novel is that despite Noa and Mozasu's contrasting aspirations they both end up working in the same profession. What differs, however, is their attitude towards their situation. For Noa, giving up his studies to work in the pachinko industry is a kind of penance for the sins of his father— and involves pretending to be Japanese. When sixteen-year-old

Mozasu takes a job in a pachinko parlour, however, it is a liberation for him. Working with other Koreans, he feels he can be completely himself and gains a sense of worth through hard work. Unashamed of how he makes his living, he is happy to be able to provide for his mother and, later, his wife and child. Going on to own his own pachinko parlours, he demonstrates that his business is as respectable as most, paying his taxes and treating his staff well. One of the key factors of Mozasu's success is his pragmatism. Although he does not believe that Japanese attitudes towards Koreans will change, he does his best with the cards that life deals him. This attitude is succinctly summed up in his reflection that "Life is shitty, but not all the time." More resilient than his brother, he refuses to be broken by circumstance. Declaring "Man, life's going to keep pushing you around, but you have to keep playing", he embodies the spirit of pachinko.

Mozasu's ability to bounce back means that, after the tragedy of Yumi's death, he eventually goes on to find love again with Etsuko. He also takes great pleasure in being able to provide his son, Solomon, with an expensive education. By sending Solomon to American schools, he aims to ensure that his son will go into a respectable profession and no one will be able to look down on him. When Solomon is fired from his investment bank, however, it becomes clear that even Mozasu's wealth cannot protect his son from prejudice against Koreans. When Solomon announces that he wants to join his father's pachinko business, Mozasu cannot help feeling disappointed. Although content to work in the business himself, he hoped for better things for his son.

Kim Changho

Kim Changho appears to be the answer to Sunja's prayers when he approaches her at the market with a business proposition. Offering excellent salaries and ideal working conditions, he asks Sunja and Kyunghee to make *kimchi* and side dishes for the chain of restaurants he manages. What Sunja does not discover until much later is that Kim Changho works for Hansu and her former lover is behind the whole scheme.

Kim Changho feels permanently indebted to Hansu as the older man rescued him when he was a boy. Before Hansu took him under his wing, he was an orphan begging on the streets. Since then, he has worked for Hansu, often carrying out his dirty work such as collecting protection money from the stall holders at the market. Hansu likes to use Kim Changho for such tasks as he is personable and respectable-looking— "he was the clean wrapper for a filthy deed."

Despite the nature of his work, Kim Changho is shown to be a decent person at heart. Over time, he becomes an indispensable source of support to Sunja's entire family. While he is in love with Kyunghee, he does not try to take advantage of Yoseb's vulnerability to win her over. Loving Kyunghee as much for her moral integrity as her beauty, he knows that she would never betray her husband. It is only when Yoseb asks Kim Changho to wait until he has died and then marry Kyunghee that he finally declares his feelings to her.

When Kyunghee refuses to consider marrying him while Yoseb is still alive, Kim Changho feels he has no reason to remain in Japan. Devastated, he leaves for North Korea, hoping to help reunify his homeland.

Pastor Yoo

Pastor Yoo runs the Hanguk Presbyterian Church in Japan where Isak becomes Associate Pastor. An elderly widower who is almost blind from cataracts, Yoo needs a deputy to help him. When Isak arrives, however, it becomes clear that the pastor has chosen him for calculated reasons. Unable to offer a half-decent salary, he knows that Isak comes from a wealthy family and is hoping for their financial support. Despite his rather mercenary reasons for hiring Isak, Yoo and his sexton live an austere life, sleeping in the office and sitting on a concrete floor to eat. Neither of them takes a salary.

Isak is initially impressed by the wise and compassionate counsel he hears Yoo give to an arguing brother and sister. He is later shocked, however, when Yoo discusses their case in a cynical manner, predicting that the siblings will end up in difficulties whatever choices they make. The incident emphasises the contrast between Isak and the pastor. While Isak is an innocent who has led a sheltered life up to this point, Yoo has seen a great deal of human suffering during his ministry to the Korean congregation and has become hardened by the experience. While he knows that, from a spiritual point of view, the young woman should decline gifts from her Japanese boss, he also realises that for Koreans in Japan, it is difficult to take the moral high ground.

Sexton Hu

Hu is a young Chinese man who was left at Pastor Yoo's church by a Japanese officer, years earlier. In the true spirit of Christianity, Yoo raised him like a son.

Hu plays a devastating role in the lives of Isak and his family when he takes a stance against the enforced ritual in which Christians are made to bow to Shinto shrines. While Pastor Yoo takes a prosaic attitude to this law (encouraging his congregation to go through the motions rather than make themselves martyrs), Hu has other ideas. Unbeknown to his mentor, he mouths the Lord's Prayer as he bows to the shrine. When challenged by a police officer, Hu boldly declares that he is no longer prepared to worship an idol. Although Hu's willingness to become a martyr for his faith shows bravery, he forces the same fate on Isak and Pastor Yoo through his association with them. All die as a result of the barbaric conditions they suffer during years of imprisonment.

Shimamura

Yoseb's employer is a ruthless man who believes himself to be soft-hearted for employing Koreans. Paying Yoseb half the salary he would have to offer a Japanese factory manager, he imposes harsh working conditions. When Isak returns home after years in prison, Yoseb knows better than to ask if he can leave early as this would be considered a sacking offence.

Shimamura does not go untouched by misfortune, as one of his sons dies in the war. This illustrates how World War II took its toll even on well-off Japanese citizens.

Sister Okja

Sister Okja is one of several Korean women in the novel who keep their families singlehandedly afloat. While her husband sits at home and drinks, Okja feeds and clothes her six children by delivering babies and babysitting in the ghetto of Ikaino.

Tamaguchi

Tamaguchi is the Japanese owner of the farm where Hansu sends Sunja and her family to escape the imminent bombing of Osaka. The potato farmer happily exploits the lack of food supplies during the war by charging extortionate prices for his produce— selling on the black market through Hansu. While the majority of the population suffer, he hides "troves of treasure" around his farm and keeps his wife in luxury.

The only downside of the war for Tamaguchi is that he loses the majority of his workforce who are sent off to fight. He takes in Sunja and her family as a favour to Hansu, expecting them to be as useless as his wife's pampered sisters. He is therefore delighted when he discovers just how hard Sunja, her sons, and Kyunghee are prepared to work.

Goro

When sixteen-year-old Mozasu punches a man for molesting a market stall holder, the intervention of Goro marks a crucial turning point in his life. Using his considerable charm, the rotund pachinko parlour owner speaks up for Mozasu's good character and the police officer lets him off with a warning. By the next day, Mozasu has quit school and is working for Goro.

Goro proves to be an important role model for Mozasu. At school, Mozasu has encountered only negative concepts of what being a Korean means. In Goro, however, he sees a successful Korean who is completely at ease with himself. Feeling no stigma about the nature of his business, Goro enjoys the fruits of his success and treats his employees well. Mozasu becomes Goro's trusted right-hand-man, working for him for years until he opens his own pachinko business.

Hoji

While Noa is studying for his university entrance exams, he works for a landlord as a bookkeeper and secretary. Although extremely wealthy, Hoji is rumoured to be Korean, or a *buraka* (from an ostracised socio-economic group known as *Burakumin*). Nevertheless, he is untroubled by the rumours— an attitude which

Noa could learn a lot from.

Haruki Totoyama

When Mozasu is thirteen, Haruki joins his class at school. Although Japanese, he lives in a deprived area bordering the Korean ghetto. This is because his younger brother, Daisuke, was born with learning disabilities and Japanese landlords view this as a curse, refusing to rent to Haruki's mother. To add to this list of unfortunate circumstances, Haruki's father is absent, abandoning his family as soon as he became aware of Daisuke's disability.

Rumours spread in school that Haruki is a *buraka* and, although he tries desperately hard to fit in, the other children shun him. After seeing Haruki rejected on numerous occasions, Mozasu allows his fellow outcast to sit with him during recess and soon begins protecting him in the school yard.

Mozasu loses touch with Haruki when he leaves school to work for Goro. They are reunited a few years later when Mozasu begins dating Yumi, who works for Haruki's mother. Now a police officer, Haruki has previously avoided bumping into Mozasu as he has always been secretly in love with him. They resume a close friendship, but Haruki never admits his true feelings to his friend.

Haruki keeps his sexuality a secret and eventually gives in to his mother's wish for him to marry her best seamstress, Ayame. Deep down he remains unhappy and continues to be troubled by the cruelty of human nature and the injustices of the world. This is illustrated when he interviews the parents of a twelve-year-old Korean boy who killed himself after being bullied by his classmates. Unable to stop thinking about it afterwards, he admits to Mozasu that he has also fought the urge to kill himself since he was a boy.

Haruki's Mother

Haruki's mother is one of many ordinary yet remarkable, women in the novel. Left a single mother when her husband rejected their disabled son, Daisuke, she juggles intensive childcare demands and running a dressmaking business. Although doctors suggest institutionalising her youngest son, she will not hear of it.

When Goro first places a uniform order with Haruki's mother

for his pachinko parlour, she is shown crying with relief at the prospect of having enough money for rent and food. As Goro's patronage leads to further orders, she moves and expands her premises, employing other seamstresses. Before dying, she ensures that Haruki marries the capable Ayame, who she knows will take care of Daisuke. After her death, Haruki is able to buy a mansion with the money his mother has saved over the years.

Akiko Fumeki

After relentlessly pursuing Noa at university, Akiko becomes his first girlfriend. In complete contrast to Noa, Akiko has radical ideas, likes to be noticed and often disagrees with the opinion of their professors. Although Noa is initially frightened of Akiko, he cannot resist her beauty and energy.

Akiko comes from an upper-class Japanese family and dating Noa forms part of her rebellion against her privileged background. With Akiko, Noa experiences discrimination in reverse as the fact that he is Korean makes him more attractive to her. Fetishizing Korean men, she assumes that they are all good looking and makes many other "positive generalizations about Koreans and other foreigners."

Accustomed to getting her own way, Akiko gate-crashes Noa's lunch with Hansu when he refuses to take her with him. Immediately, she sees what Noa has failed to pick up on—the telling physical resemblance between the two men. Taking in Hansu's obvious wealth, she comes to the conclusion that Noa is ashamed of the fact that his father is a *yakuza*. In the ensuing argument, she drops the double bombshell, having no idea of the devastating impact her words will have on her boyfriend.

Noa breaks up with Akiko realising that she cannot see beyond her exotic idea of what a Korean is. Her determination to see him as a "good Korean" is just as dehumanising as being looked down upon because of his race. Noa also sees that Akiko's relationship with him allows her to feel good about herself, as "she had condescended to be with someone everyone else hated." As such, it will never be a relationship of equals.

Professor Kuroda

When Noa is a student at Waseda University, his scholarly nature is illustrated by the fact that he always sits at the front during Professor Kuroda's English literature lectures. Akiko jokes that the elderly academic is in love with Noa and Professor Kuroda is clearly hurt when he starts sitting at the back of the lecture hall with his girlfriend.

In a lecture focusing on the novels of George Eliot, Professor Kuroda raises a number of themes which are also pertinent to *Pachinko*. Firstly, she points out that in Eliot's novels "a woman's lot" is "determined by her economic position and marriage prospects" —a viewpoint echoed earlier in Lee's novel by Jun's wife. Secondly, the professor discusses Eliot's character, Daniel Deronda, suggesting that Daniel's discovery that he is Jewish liberates him to marry Mirah—another Jewish character. Significantly, Noa responds hostilely to this second point, disliking the implication that Daniel should marry someone from the same persecuted minority. His reaction foreshadows the fact that he will go on to deny his origins and marry a Japanese woman.

Yumi

Absorbed by his work, Mozasu is uninterested in relationships with women until he meets Yumi. At the workshop owned by Haruki's mother, Yumi is the only seamstress who does not fawn over Mozasu when he comes to be fitted for a suit. When Mozasu asks her out to dinner she declares that she has no time for such "nonsense" and is going to an English night class instead. Unimpressed by material things, Yumi has a passion for learning that is reminiscent of Noa.

Yumi's aloof manner arises from a fear that people will discover her shameful origins. As parents go, she is dealt the worst possible start in life—her mother is a prostitute with an alcohol addiction and her father is a violent pimp. At the age of fourteen, she ran away from home with her youngest sister. Sleeping in a disused clothing factory, Yumi supported them both by working in textile factories until her sister died of a fever.

For Yumi, being a Korean in Japan is "just another horrible encumbrance, much like being poor or having a shameful family you could not cast off." Learning English is the first part of her plan to move to the United States: a place which she believes is more accepting of difference.

Mozasu wheedles his way into Yumi's affections by attending the English night class with her and showing off the English vocabulary he learned from Noa. Their marriage is a happy one until Yumi is killed by a drunk driver while pushing their son to safety. After her death, Mozasu feels guilty about persuading Yumi to remain in Japan, wishing he had fulfilled her dream of moving to the United States.

John Maryman

John Maryman is the teacher of the English night class attended by Mozasu and Yumi. Although Korean, he was adopted as a baby by wealthy American missionaries when his biological parents left him with their landlord.

Despite being abandoned, life turned out well for John, as his adopted parents were loving and could afford to educate him at Yale and Princeton. To his credit, he chooses to swap his comfortable existence in the USA for teaching English to Koreans in Japan. Feeling that his own life has been blessed, John pities his students. By teaching them "another language that wasn't Japanese" he hopes to boost their self-esteem and improve their chances in life. Although he is a Presbyterian pastor, he makes no attempt to preach to his students, instead engaging them with humour.

Mieko

When Sunja goes to Hansu's house (hoping for news of Noa) she encounters Mieko, Hansu's Japanese wife. In her early sixties but still beautiful, Mieko decides that Sunja is not pretty enough to be her husband's mistress and assumes that she is a beggar. She tells her servant to give Sunja food and then send her away.

In her encounter with Sunja, Mieko displays patronising ideas about Korean personality traits, reflecting "Koreans could be insistent like unruly children." Despite being married to a Korean (and having half-Korean children), she still does not view them as individuals.

Mieko is hugely wealthy thanks to her marriage, but her husband was the choice of her father. Their partnership is civil but distant.

Hideo Takano

Hideo Takano is the Japanese manager of Cosmos Pachinko—a chain of pachinko parlours in Nagano. Takano has a strict policy of refusing to hire Koreans and makes Noa swear that he is not a "foreigner" before he employs him. In reality, Takano suspects that Noa is Korean but takes a liking to him, deciding that it does not matter as long as no one else finds out. This suggests that Takano's racist employment policies have been created to cater to the prejudices of other people.

Solomon

Solomon is the son of Mozasu and Yumi and is only three and a half when his mother dies. Nevertheless, he is a cheerful child who benefits from the compassion that people who know about his mother's death feel for him.

Right from birth, Solomon's family have optimistic expectations of him. When Yoseb chooses the name Solomon for his great-nephew, he is thinking of biblical Solomon: a wise man and king. Meanwhile, Mozasu hopes that his son will grow up to be "an international man of the world." Using his considerable wealth to ensure this happens, Mozasu sends Solomon to an international school where only English is spoken. Here Solomon mixes as an equal with the children of wealthy Americans and Europeans, sheltered from the prejudice against Koreans that he would inevitably face in a Japanese school.

The first blot on Solomon's apparently charmed life comes when he must go through the humiliating process of alien registration on his fourteenth birthday. This is a legal requirement that Mozasu's money cannot protect his son from. Significantly, during his lavish birthday party afterwards, Solomon still has the hint of an ink stain on his fingers, despite washing his hands.

Going to college in New York, Solomon is again in an environment where he is free from Japanese prejudice. In the United States, Koreans are considered hard-working "model citizens" and during his studies, he acquires a Korean-American girlfriend. Solomon fulfils his father's dream when he moves back to Japan and starts working for Travis Brothers—a British-owned investment bank. Boasting employees from all over the world, it seems precisely the kind of international, non-prejudiced environment that Mozasu has always hoped his son would excel in. Solomon's world comes crashing down, however, when his Japanese boss demonstrates his prejudices in the most insidious way. Exploiting Solomon's Korean connections to secure a real estate deal, he then fires him, implying that the bank cannot afford to be associated with Korean *yakuza*.

Losing his job proves to be a crucial turning point for Solomon. An obvious solution to the problem would be to return to the United States, marry his long-term girlfriend and, in so doing, acquire American citizenship. While this solution would make both his girlfriend and Mozasu happy, Solomon realises that he is not prepared to marry Phoebe and he does not want to be an American citizen.

Solomon's decision to break up with Phoebe is based on his increasing discomfort at her anti-Japanese stance. Although we might expect him to endorse Phoebe's views after the experience with his Japanese boss, Solomon does not forget that many of the people he loves (Etsuko, Hana, Haruki etc.) are Japanese. He also believes that he has the right to call himself Japanese—even if Japanese law does not recognise this.

While his father encourages him to apply for a job at another bank, Solomon chooses to follow in Mozasu's footsteps in the pachinko business. Mozasu is disappointed and Solomon's decision has echoes of the moment Noa gives up university to work for a pachinko parlour. Noa's decision, however, is a nihilistic one, driven by the belief that he has no future, while Solomon's choice is one that leaves room for hope. Despite having more opportunities than his father and uncle, he elects to stay in Japan and work in the pachinko business because he feels it is the right path for him. Although knowing that he will never be a fully integrated citizen in Japan, he remains, confident in his own right to be there. Given the choice of working in more respected professions, he chooses pachinko, knowing that it is as respectable a business as many others.

Noriko

When Hansu hires the hostess, Noriko, she is pleased to be chosen as the older man has a reputation for buying hostesses expensive gifts. Their date does not go as she anticipates, however, when Hansu leaves her in the car while he attends Yumi's funeral. Bored of waiting, she sends the driver to fetch his master, announcing that she wants to go shopping. Enraged at being interrupted, Hansu launches a vicious assault on Noriko, hitting her repeatedly in the face.

After the attack, Hansu continues with his day as normal, returning to his office, while Noriko's life is ruined. Even after plastic surgery, she is no longer attractive enough to work in the hostess bar. Her only option is to work in a Turkish bath where she must bathe and service naked men.

Risa Iwamura

When his boss urges him to marry, Noa identifies Risa as a suitable candidate. A reserved Japanese filing clerk, she dresses to evade rather than attract attention. Noa, however, is drawn to Risa's beautiful handwriting and by the fact that she is generally considered unmarriageable. Although born into a respectable middle-class family, she carries the burden of parental disgrace. When Risa was a teenager, her father (a doctor) accidentally administered the wrong medicine to two of his patients. The patients died, and Dr Iwamura took his own life, leaving his family destitute. Like Noa, Risa understands the shame that can be inflicted by one's parents and the way this can taint the future.

Noa feels affection for his wife but does not love her with the passion he felt for Akiko. Despite having four children with her, he does not tell Risa that he is Korean. When Noa commits suicide, Risa is left to face disgrace all over again.

Risa's Mother

Risa's mother is unhappy about her daughter marrying Noa as he works in the pachinko business—a fact that will seal "her caste in life." She also correctly suspects that he might be Korean. Nevertheless, she secretly has a soft spot for Noa as his melancholy aura reminds her of her dead husband. This turns out to be a spookily perceptive observation as her son-in-law, like her husband, goes on to take his own life.

Ayame

Ayame works as a seamstress for Haruki's mother who, having observed her employee's capable nature, is keen for her to marry her son. Having given up on finding a husband, Ayame is happy to comply. After they marry, and Haruki's mother falls ill with stomach cancer, Ayame takes over the running of the business, as well as caring for Haruki's younger brother, Daisuke. When Haruki's mother dies, it is Ayame's decision to sell the dressmaking shop and move to Yokohama.

Ayame devotes herself to caring for her husband's younger brother who, although now thirty, has the mental age of a young child. Her only respite is when a special education teacher visits Daisuke. It is then that she goes shopping and to the public baths. During these afternoons, Ayame gets into the habit of walking through a park where couples meet for sex. Watching these couplings reminds Ayame of the intimacy that is missing from her own stable, yet passionless, marriage. Haruki ceased making love to her after their attempts to conceive a child were unsuccessful and they discovered she was infertile. One day Ayame discovers the real reason for her husband's lack of ardour when she sees him in the park having sex with another man. Feeling unlovable, she almost gives in to the advances of a beautiful young woman but changes her mind when the girl demands to see her money.

On her return home, Ayame says nothing to her husband about what she saw in the park. Readers are left to ponder how the rest of their marriage will pan out with both parties keeping silent about their secrets.

Etsuko Nagatomi

After Yumi's death, Mozasu eventually begins dating Etsuko—a forty-two-year-old Japanese divorcee who owns her own restaurant. Etsuko has three children but her adult sons will have nothing to do with her and her relationship with her daughter is strained. This is because Etsuko committed adultery while she was married to their father—unthinkable behaviour for a woman in Japanese society. As a result, her children have been tainted with the shame of her actions and have become social outcasts. Etsuko gives up all claim to custody of her children, feeling she has been a failure as a mother, but grieves over the loss.

Etsuko's mother and sister disapprove of her relationship with Mozasu due to his race and his profession. Mozasu wants to marry her but Etsuko's mother insists that to marry "a pachinko Korean" would heap further shame on her children. This leaves Etsuko in a no-win situation. While she refuses to give up Mozasu, who she loves fiercely, she will not accept his repeated marriage proposals for fear of hurting her children further. Her distress when Mozasu presents her with "a mistress watch" (as she will not accept an engagement ring) illustrates her conflicted priorities.

Etsuko demonstrates her essentially good heart in her relationships with Hana and Solomon. Fearful of disrupting her already fragile relationship with her daughter, she tiptoes round Hana, trying to keep her safe while feeling she can exert very little influence. With Solomon, her relationship is less complicated, and she is as loving and supportive as any biological mother.

Hana

Etsuko's fifteen-year-old daughter, Hana, comes to stay with her mother when she discovers she is pregnant. Afraid to tell her father, she expects Etsuko to help her out of the predicament.

Hana is not the first teenage girl to become pregnant in *Pachinko*. Her considerable sexual experience and provocative style of dressing, however, contrast sharply with Sunja's innocence when she falls pregnant by Hansu. While petulance, mood-swings and unpredictability are not unusual teenage characteristics, in Hana they are exaggerated to extreme levels. A mixture of hard cynicism and vulnerability, she shows herself to be needy of her mother's love and care one moment and kicks against it the next. Nine years old when her parents divorced, she is clearly still deeply damaged by the impact, taking refuge in addictions to sex and alcohol.

Hana's self-destructive urges make her a danger to herself and others. Fourteen-year-old Solomon does not stand a chance against her plan to seduce him and he is immediately besotted. While Solomon dreams of them marrying once he is old enough, however, Hana has a different agenda. Hoping to be a porn star (as she realises that she doesn't have the talent for mainstream stardom), she makes Solomon practice a variety of sexual scenarios to perfect her art. Always dictating the terms of their relationship, she takes money from him until he has no more. She then leaves him devastated when she departs for Tokyo without warning.

Hana becomes a hostess in Tokyo, but her alcohol addiction causes her to lose job after job. Although she dreams of Solomon coming to rescue her, she continues to play games with him, calling but refusing to reveal where she is. At college with a new girlfriend, Solomon still wants to rescue Hana but knows, deep down, that she is a lost cause.

When Etsuko finally traces Hana through a private investigator, she is working in a Turkish bath and has contracted the HIV virus. By the time Solomon goes to see her in hospital, she is dying of AIDS. Solomon urges Hana to go to America for more advanced treatment. Hana, however, makes it clear that she feels she deserves her fate and does not want to live. Despite treating Solomon badly, he is the only man she ever really loved. Before dying, she advises Solomon to take over his father's pachinko business.

Phoebe

When Solomon moves back to Japan after studying in New York, he is accompanied by his Korean-American girlfriend, Phoebe. Phoebe feels isolated and unhappy in Tokyo as she cannot get a work visa and does not speak Japanese. Having lived in the United States all her life, she is taken aback by the racism and social inequalities suffered by Koreans in Japan. This leads her to take an anti-Japanese stance which Solomon feels uncomfortable with.

Living in Japan crushes Phoebe's spirit and, when she realises that Solomon does not want to marry her, she returns to the USA. Her viewpoint bears similarities to the author's own experiences. Living in Tokyo for several years when her husband worked for an investment bank, Min Jin Lee felt homesick and cut off from her family.

Giancarlo

An Italian who has lived in Japan for some time, Giancarlo works at Travis Brothers. When Solomon starts beating him at poker, Giancarlo brings up the fact that Mozasu is a pachinko parlour owner (implying that Solomon comes from a rich but disreputable background). This is Solomon's first experience of casual but inherent prejudice. Disconcerted, he deliberately loses the game.

Kazu

When Solomon begins working at the investment bank, Travis Brothers, he believes he has the ideal boss. Japanese but educated in America, Kazu appears unprejudiced against Koreans. Expressing anger at the way Korean people have been treated in Japan, he declares to Solomon that "you people should have a revolution."

Kazu appears to show favouritism towards Solomon when he asks him to join an elite team who are trying to secure a real estate deal for a client. His real plan, however, is to exploit Solomon's Korean connections. Solomon falls straight into Kazu's hands, enlisting the help of his father and Goro. As Kazu anticipates, a Korean woman who refuses to sell her property to the Japanese sells it to Goro who is respected within the Korean community. When the seller dies shortly afterwards, however, Kazu shows his true colours, implying that Goro and Mozasu are *yakuza* and somehow involved in her death. Making Solomon a scapegoat, he fires him, claiming he must protect the bank's reputation.

Sonoko Matsuda

When ninety-three-year-old Sonoko Matsuda refuses to sell her property, she potentially stands in the way of the building of a premiere golf course. A Korean who lost her children when they returned to their homeland and died there, she will not sell to a Japanese buyer at any price.

THEMES & IMAGERY

Curses and Fate

When Noa and his family visit Matsumoto Castle, a guide tells them the story of Tada Kasuke's curse which, according to legend, caused the castle to tilt for two hundred years. Transfixed, Noa's young son, Koichi, asks what a curse is and how it can be reversed. In raising this question, Koichi touches on a central concern of Lee's novel.

Many of the characters in *Pachinko* are born into seemingly cursed circumstances. When Noa wearily tells Koichi that it isn't easy to reverse a curse, he is thinking of his own inability to escape the identity of his biological father. Noa, however, is not the first of his family to be born with the burden of misfortune. The chain begins with Noa's grandfather, Hoonie, who is born with a cleft palate and a twisted foot—physical defects which seriously impair his chances of marrying. Although Hoonie does go on to find a wife and have a healthy daughter, the "curse" filters down to Sunja whose marriage prospects are also damaged by the fact that she may pass on her father's genes to her children.

For the Korean characters, the notion of being cursed is linked to their national identity. Throughout the novel, Koreans have to choose between two equally undesirable options—to face persecution in their own country or be treated as second-class citizens in Japan. The additional burdens that they carry, through no fault of their own, emphasise just how far the decks are stacked against them. Yumi, for example, who is the daughter of an alcoholic prostitute and a violent pimp, is no more responsible for her parentage than she is for her nationality and sees being Korean as "just another horrible encumbrance".

Cursed existences are not, however, the sole preserve of the Koreans in the novel. Several Japanese characters are also shown to be shunned by society for circumstances that are beyond their control. Although Mozasu's school friend, Haruki, is Japanese, his family is forced to live in a deprived area near the Korean ghetto. This is because his younger brother, Daisuke, was born with learning disabilities which are regarded as a curse in Japanese society. This misfortune not only stops Japanese landlords from renting to them but also sends Daisuke's father running for the hills as soon as his son is born. Also stigmatised is Noa's wife, Risa, who carries the burden of parental disgrace. Despite being born into a respectable middle-class family, she is considered unmarriageable as her father killed himself after accidentally causing the deaths of two of his patients. Meanwhile, Etsuko's children become "village outcasts" when their mother's adultery is discovered. No longer sharing the rosy prospects of other middle-class Japanese children, the boys fail in college while Hana descends into alcoholism and sex work. Every one of these cases illustrates the narrow-mindedness of Japanese society and its devastating impact on those who fall foul of it.

The idea of a cursed destiny seems to be borne out in the fates of certain characters. Although offered hope in the shape of second chances, they seem unable to shake off their misfortune. Noa is presented with a second chance at life when he marries and has a family, but still feels "the story of his life as a Korean like a dark, heavy rock within him." Overcoming her dysfunctional origins, Yumi finds happiness and starts her own family with Mozasu but dies tragically young. Perhaps cruellest of all is the fate of Risa whose story has the doom-laden inevitability of a Greek tragedy. Having escaped the disgrace of her father's suicide and created a family with Noa, she and her children face shame once again when her husband takes his own life.

Lee's focus on the idea of fate and curses in *Pachinko* powerfully brings home the fact that life can be cruel and there is little natural justice in the world. On the other hand, she also makes it clear that some "curses" can be self-fulfilling. While Hana and Noa are very different characters, the author shows that, once they believe their lives to be blighted, they both set out on self-destructive paths, cutting themselves off from any hope of rescue. When Noa discovers that Hansu is his father, he takes a road that he knows can never lead to happiness. Hana, meanwhile, believes she is innately bad and goes on to act in a way that ensures bad things happen to her. Although the characters who fight their fates may not always succeed, those who give in to them stand no chance at all.

Resilience

Pachinko begins with the line "History has failed us, but no matter." This statement neatly sums up the attitude of many of the Korean characters in Lee's novel. Historically, they have been faced with continual hardship and persecution. Nevertheless, they continue with their lives, regardless of these obstacles. While there are many aspects of life that they have no control of, Lee's characters are rarely passive victims, constantly adapting and taking action with each new challenge.

It is no accident that the novel begins with an act of resilience. Faced with steep tax raises imposed by the colonial government, Hoonie's parents respond by sleeping in the anteroom of their kitchen and renting out their bedroom to lodgers. This marks the beginnings of their boarding house—a business which they pass on to their son.

Although the male characters in the novel face many challenges, it is the resilience of the female characters that Lee particularly celebrates. While raised in a culture where a woman's fate is thought to be largely determined by her husband's economic status, the women in the novel frequently rely on their own resourcefulness to support themselves and their children. When Hoonie dies, Yangjin has no time for prolonged grieving as she takes over the running of the boarding house. When Isak is imprisoned, Sunja cannot afford to sit around waiting for his release and begins hawking at the market. Meanwhile, Kyunghee cooks *kimchi* around the clock, at first to supplement Yoseb's wages, and later, to support him when his accident leaves him unable to work.

Lee brings home just how remarkable the women's achievements are by focusing on the relentless hard work that goes into them. Yangjin ensures that her boarding house is always full by pampering her lodgers and conjuring up tasty meals with meagre ingredients (often scrimping on her own portions to offer the greedy Fatso seconds). To keep this service running efficiently involves an endless cycle of cooking, cleaning and laundering.

Sunja's job as a hawker demands stamina and bravery, involving long hours and exposure to both the elements and the general public. Similarly inspiring is the perseverance shown by Haruki's mother—a single parent who runs a dressmaking business while caring for her disabled son. Motivated by a determination to take care of their loved ones, these ordinary and yet extraordinary women juggle long hours of work and childcare and are successful in their enterprises.

Women like Sunja and Haruki's mother, who tirelessly battle for survival, do not necessarily pass this resilience on to their children. Although Mozasu inherits his mother's fighting spirit, Noa does not and, ultimately, it is his inability to bounce back from adversity that leads to his death. Haruki, meanwhile, is a melancholic figure who struggles to move beyond his childhood traumas. By contrasting the characters of Mozasu and Haruki, Lee emphasises the vital role of resilience in an individual's future. While the childhood friends suffer similar bullying at school, and both feel like killing themselves at the time, the impact on their later lives differs significantly. Mozasu succeeds in moving on but the more sensitive Haruki continues to be haunted by the cruelty he suffered and still frequently considers suicide.

Sacrifice

Faced with social and economic challenges, the characters in *Pachinko* are forced to make difficult choices. In several cases, this results in a personal sacrifice of some kind. Many of the most strikingly selfless acts in the novel are made by women—emphasised in the repeated refrain, "A woman's lot is to suffer".

On several occasions, mothers are shown to make sacrifices for their children. When Sunja becomes pregnant without a father in sight, Yangjin has to choose between keeping her child and grandchild close to her (although both will be disgraced) or encouraging Sunja's marriage to Isak. For her daughter's sake, Yangjin chooses the latter course of action without hesitation. The pain this decision causes her, however, is illustrated in the heart-breaking scene where she packs Sunja's suitcase ready for her to leave for Japan. Yangjin's eagerness to pack as many goodies in as possible reflects her realisation that she may never see her daughter again.

Later in the novel, Sunja is faced with a maternal dilemma when Noa earns a place at Waseda University. Although illiterate herself, she is determined to help her son fulfil his dream of becoming a scholar. Unable to fund his studies, however, she must accept Hansu's financial assistance to do so. For Sunja, who has supported her boys single-handedly up to this point, this involves sacrificing her pride, as well as opening the door to allow Hansu into her son's life. Again, the internal debate before the decision is made is a short one, as Sunja cannot consider standing in the way of her son's education.

Mozasu's girlfriend, Etsuko, is another example of a woman who has made considerable sacrifices for her children. In her case, this initially involves the painful decision to give up custody of them without a fight. After committing adultery, Etsuko knows she has very little chance of keeping her children and tries to minimise the disruption to their lives by going quietly. Later, she makes a further painful decision when she refuses to marry Mozasu to spare her children further shame. Etsuko, like Yangjin and Sunja, bases these decisions on maternal instincts which compel her to put her children's welfare before her own.

While maternal love is a powerful factor, it is not only the mothers in the novel who make significant personal sacrifices. Childless women are also shown to possess this selfless instinct. Haruki's wife, Ayame, for example, devotes herself to caring for her husband's mentally disabled brother, Daisuke. Meanwhile, Kyunghee—probably the most selfless character in the novel—spends her life caring for others, including Sunja's children and mother, and her own husband. Offered a chance of happiness when her dying husband gives his blessing for her to marry Kim Changho, she refuses to even consider it while Yoseb is still alive.

It is interesting to note that, while the women of the novel make sacrifices out of love, the male characters are more inclined to do so out of faith or idealism. Isak's utter selflessness comes from belief in God and a desire to do good in the world. Initially refusing himself the luxury of considering marriage (as he does not want to leave a widow in the world), he changes his mind when he sees the opportunity to avert the disgrace of Sunja and her unborn child. Lee shows similarly noble characteristics in John Maryman— a Yale educated minister who leaves his comfortable existence in the United States to teach English to less fortunate Koreans in

Japan. Sexton Hu makes an even greater sacrifice in the name of faith when he is imprisoned for refusing to worship at a Shinto shrine. Noa, meanwhile, sacrifices his happiness after discovering Hansu's true identity. Believing that his education has been funded by corrupt means, he abandons his university degree—and with it, his dreams.

Although many acts of sacrifice occur in *Pachinko*, very few of them are rewarded. By allowing Hansu to fund Noa's university expenses, Sunja sets into motion a chain of events that will lead to her son's suicide. Kyunghee is lonely for many years after nobly rejecting Kim Changho's proposal. Etsuko's children continue to make her pay for her earlier transgressions. Sexton Hu's act of martyrdom condemns Isak and Pastor Yoo to death. And Noa's decision to give up his education is a dramatic gesture, but readers are left to question what anyone gains from it. In Lee's fictional world there is no sense of karma or "what goes around comes around". Instead, readers are presented with a realistic (if rather dispiriting) picture of the true nature of sacrifice.

Prejudice

When Sunja first arrives in Japan, she is shocked by the conditions in which her brother-in-law and his wife are living. Although Yoseb has a responsible job, he and Kyunghee are living in a slum-like ghetto—a far cry from their comfortable middle-class backgrounds in Korea. This marks the beginning of Sunja's realisation that, in Japan, Koreans languish at the very bottom of the social strata. Relegated the worst housing, they have no chance of entering certain professions and are inadequately paid for the jobs they are permitted to do.

Perpetually cast in the role of unwelcome outsiders, even second- and third-generation Koreans in Japan are branded as *Zainichi* (a word which literally translates to "foreign resident staying in Japan"). Thus, Solomon, whose father was born in Japan, still has to go through the process of alien registration with the possibility of deportation. Lee illustrates how the Japanese refusal to accept them as full citizens provokes a sense of shame in the Korean characters. This is particularly evident in Noa who is ashamed of his Korean origins from early childhood. No matter how hard he tries to be a model Korean, however, his efforts are never enough to gain acceptance.

While Japan is portrayed as a xenophobic nation, its prejudices are not restricted to race. Several non-Koreans in the novel are also the victims of the discriminatory nature of Japanese society. A number of characters are made social outcasts by contravening Japanese standards of behaviour. Etsuko, for example, becomes a social pariah when she commits adultery, while Risa's father takes his own life—an act that is considered particularly shameful in Japanese society. In these cases, it is not just the perpetrator who is ostracised but the entire family.

Through some of the more minor characters, Lee also illustrates residual class prejudices inherited from Japan's former feudal caste system. Just one rung up the social order from Koreans are *Burakumin*—Japan's equivalent of "untouchables". A socio-economic group, rather than a race, *Burakumin* were the descendants of *Eta* (literally meaning "abundance of filth"). Eta were so called as they performed jobs which were considered to be impure, such as leather tanning, butchery and undertaking. Significantly, when Sunja first goes to Osaka market to sell *kimchi*, the only vacant spot she can find is beside a butcher (who would almost certainly be perceived as a *buraka*). Mozasu's friend, Haruki, is also shunned by his Japanese classmates due to the belief that his family is *Burakumin*. This rumour spreads because Haruki lives in the poor Japanese district which borders the Korean ghetto. The truth is, however, that Haruki's family live in this area due to a different kind of discrimination. As the learning disabilities of Haruki's younger brother are interpreted as a curse, the majority of landlords refuse to rent to them.

Throughout the novel, Lee demonstrates the self-perpetuating nature of prejudice. Labelling Koreans as "filthy", the Japanese ensure that this is a reality by forcing them to live in cramped, unhygienic conditions. The perception of Koreans as dishonest and morally deficient is backed up by pointing out their involvement in immoral moneymaking schemes (organised crime and pachinko parlours). This stereotyping glosses over the fact that the moral high ground is an unaffordable luxury for a minority who are disadvantaged in almost every area of life.

In the limited options available to her characters, Lee illustrates the vicious circle that many Korean immigrants find themselves in as they are driven to fulfil Japanese stereotypes. While Hansu is the only genuine *yakuza*, other characters are shown to be morally compromised by their situations. Perhaps the most striking example of this is Kim Changho—a good-hearted man who, nevertheless, carries out much of Hansu's dirty work, including collecting protection fees and trading on the black market. The disconnect between his character and his profession is explained when we learn Kim Changho feels indebted to Hansu as he rescued him from begging on the streets as a child.

By showing the impact of discrimination on its characters, *Pachinko* emphasises the resilience that is required to face prejudice on a day-to-day basis. As Isak says to Noa "Living every day in the presence of those who refuse to acknowledge your humanity takes great courage." Powerfully illustrating the way that prejudice dehumanises its victims, Lee tries to redress the balance by ensuring that her characters are fully-fleshed and sympathetic.

Identity & Home

Throughout *Pachinko,* there is a strong sense that blood establishes who you are. This idea relates not only to the characters' parentage but also to their nationality. For the Korean characters, nationality firmly establishes their place in life, dictating the way they are treated and restricting their opportunities.

For Koreans living in Japan, identity is inevitably linked with the sense of shame associated with being treated as a second-class citizen. They are also faced with a choice between two opposing identities—the "good" or the "bad Korean". "Good" Koreans like Noa and Isak face the daunting task of proving prejudice to be unjust by becoming model citizens. Meanwhile, "Bad" Koreans, like Hansu and Mozasu decide that there is no point in fighting a rigged system and fulfil the stereotypes that the Japanese expect of them.

Pushed into rigid identity templates, the Korean characters are also stripped of any clear sense of home or belonging. Colonisation, migration and war fracture their sense of who they are. In Japan, Koreans never feel completely "at home" as they are not fully accepted into Japanese society. Their sense of Korea as home also becomes increasingly flimsy, however, as their homeland is colonised, divided and then torn apart by civil war. First-generation migrants Sunja and Kyunghee still think of Korea as home but are prevented from returning, first by the privation caused by colonial rule and then by the Korean War. By the end of the war, the country they yearn for no longer exists. Remaining in Japan, they are then officially labelled as South Korean, despite the fact that their country was unified when they left it.

While Sunja and Kyunghee yearn for home, Hansu and Yoseb are shown to identify with no nation in particular. Hansu has no interest in who wins the Korean War or World War II. His only concern is how the outcome will affect him personally. Meanwhile, Yoseb feels neither loyalty to Japan nor a sentimental attachment towards Korea, believing in protecting the family unit above all else. When Kyunghee wants to socialise with their Korean neighbours in the ghetto, Yoseb warns her not to become involved stating, "Just because they're Korean doesn't mean they're our friends."

For the second-generation migrants in the novel such as Mozasu and Noa, the concept of home is even more distant. Born in Japan, Sunja's sons have never set foot on Korean soil and yet neither of them feels accepted as a Japanese citizen. With no nostalgic memories of Korea to fall back on, they are left trying to find their place in a society that is essentially hostile towards them. After abandoning his life as a good Korean, Noa tries to shed his national identity completely by passing himself off as Japanese. This plan is successful on the surface, but the denial of his true self involves constant deception and ultimately leads him to an even greater sense of dislocation. By contrast, Mozasu uses the few advantages his national identity gives him by entering the Korean-dominated pachinko business and becoming a wealthy man. Although never feeling accepted by Japanese society and dreaming of moving to Korea, he finds a secure sense of self in his family and his work.

In raising Solomon, Mozasu tries to ensure that his son will be able to choose his identity and the place that he calls home. Sending him to international schools and to college in the USA, he gives Solomon the chance to escape both Japan and the stigma attached to his Korean blood. Although his father's wealth protects him from a certain amount of discrimination, Solomon still has to go through alien registration—a humiliating reminder that the Japanese do not consider him to be at home in their country. Nevertheless, given the option to marry Phoebe and become an

American citizen, he decides to stay in Japan. Importantly, Solomon makes this decision fully aware that he will never be fully assimilated into Japanese society. In doing so, he shows that he is willing to embrace his heritage as a Korean rather than attempt to escape from it.

Parent-Child Relationships

The intensity of parental love is emphasised from the start of *Pachinko*. Worrying about their son's future as the "neighbourhood cripple", Hoonie's ageing parents do all they can to ensure he is able to look after himself when they are gone. Hoonie, in turn, dotes on Sunja, marvelling that he had a hand in creating such a perfect child. Likewise, when Sunja becomes a mother, the love she feels for her boys throws all other relationships into the shade.

Many of the characters lose babies, making any surviving children seem even more precious. Yangjin has six miscarriages before Sunja is born and Yumi has two before the birth of Solomon. Lee also conveys the sense of loss experienced by women who are unable to have children of their own. Kyunghee and Ayame are both infertile and channel their maternal instincts into other peoples' children—Kyunghee does so by minding Noa and Mozasu while Daisuke becomes a surrogate child to Ayame, even though he is a grown man.

As well as celebrating the intensity of the parent-child bond, Min Jin Lee is brutally honest about the suffering that this relationship can bring to both sides. On several occasions, parents are shown to make excruciatingly difficult choices concerning the welfare of their children. The biological parents of John Maryman abandon him as a baby, leaving him with their landlord. While this seems like a gross act of parental neglect, John's adoptive mother suggests that it was an act of sacrifice and love—unable to feed or clothe their son, they left him with someone who could. Etsuko is also shown to give up her children at great personal cost. Wanting to protect them from further hurt and shame after she commits adultery, she gives up all claim to custody. Still, however, she feels that "Being a mother was what defined her more than any other thing". Although Etsuko re-establishes a fragile relationship with Hana when her daughter seeks her help to arrange an abortion, she loses her again—first when she disappears to Tokyo and then when she dies of AIDS.

Central to the novel are the dilemmas faced by Sunja concerning Noa's future. It is with Noa's best interests in mind that she allows Hansu to pay for Noa's education, but it is a decision that costs her dearly. When Noa discovers that Hansu is his real father, he cuts himself off from both of them, leaving Sunja feeling as if she is "half-dead". Years later, when Hansu finally traces Noa, Sunja faces another unbearable choice. Should she approach her son, or respect his wish not to be contacted? As soon as she catches a glimpse of Noa, she is compelled to make contact but her impulsive actions lead to his suicide.

The pain caused by the parent-child relationship is not confined to parental suffering. Much of the novel explores the negative impact of parents on their children. At the extreme end of this scale is Yumi's mother—a prostitute and alcoholic who beats and neglects her children. Even well-meaning and loving parents, however, are shown to inadvertently cause their children suffering. No matter how deeply Sunja loves Noa, she cannot make up for the fact that he is the illegitimate child of Hansu. Etsuko's children remain social outcasts, despite the sacrifices she makes for them. Meanwhile, Noa leaves his own children disgraced and fatherless when he takes his own life. In this way, the novel illustrates the cycle of love and pain that inevitably accompanies the complex parent-child bond.

Love and Marriage

In the course of her novel, Lee presents many different examples of love and marriage. Avoiding romanticising the subject, she investigates the different types of love and affection that may exist between couples, raising interesting questions about what makes a good or bad marriage.

Although there are passionate relationships in the novel, few of them lead to long-term commitment. As a young woman, Sunja believes herself to be in love with Hansu but is prevented from marrying him by the inconvenient existence of another wife. Noa is passionately in love with Akiko but cuts her out of his life when he realises that she is attracted to the novelty of his nationality. Solomon also falls head over heels for Hana and, as a teenager, is all set to marry her as soon as he is old enough. He is saved from this fate, however, when she disappears. While these relationships are electrified by the passion of youth, there is also the sense that marriage would prove disastrous for all concerned.

Of all the marriages in the novel, only two are conventional love matches. The romance between Mozasu and Yumi blossoms into a marriage which is both respectful and loving— only brought to an end by Yumi's death. Also based on attraction and mutual devotion is the marriage of Yoseb and Kyunghee. This love, however, does not ensure blissful happiness. Yoseb's wish to protect and care for his wife is shown to restrict her liberty and ambitions. While they never cease to love each other, Kyunghee also feels increasingly lonely as Yoseb withdraws into himself after Isak's death.

Many of the marriages in *Pachinko* are represented as compromises of one sort or another— some of them more successful than others. Hansu and his Japanese wife, Mieko marry to please Mieko's father. Both parties benefit—Hansu gains prestige, while Mieko is kept in luxury—but their relationship is civil rather than affectionate. By immediately bathing after sex with her husband, Mieko signals her distaste for the activity and, after their daughters are born, Hansu meets his sexual needs with other women. Another marriage engineered by a parent is that of Haruki and Ayame. Recognising that Ayame will be both a good wife and a diligent carer for her disabled son, Daisuke, Haruki's mother pressurises her son into marriage. Haruki is a considerate husband and Ayame the model wife but it is a bloodless marriage. Lonely and sexually frustrated, Ayame only realises why her husband avoids bedroom encounters when she comes across him having sex with another man. Meanwhile, Haruki continues to carry a torch for his lifelong friend, Mozasu. Noa's marriage to Risa is also shown to be a compromise—although one he chooses for himself. The marriage is based on affection rather than passion and, by lying to his Risa about his origins, Noa conceals his true self from his wife.

It is interesting to note that two of the most harmonious marriages in the novel are between couples who barely know each other when they become man and wife. Yangjin has never laid eyes on Hoonie until the day she marries him. Although the marriage is arranged out of financial necessity (on Yangjin's side) and is not based on passionate love, it brings quiet contentment to both parties. Hoonie cannot believe his good fortune in finding a good-natured wife who bears him a perfect child. Meanwhile, Yangjin comes to realise that providence has delivered a husband with truly special qualities. Sunja's marriage to Isak follows a similar pattern as, pregnant by a married man, she finds herself in circumstances where only marriage can save her. Isak's proposal is motivated not by love but by a wish to do good in the world and neither one of them has any idea how their life together will work out. Although Sunja remains infatuated with Hansu, she grows to love her gentle husband and they develop an intimacy. They are also shown to make a good team as Sunja's practicality balances Isak's admirable (but often impractical) idealism.

Through many of the relationships between men and women in *Pachinko,* there is a common thread of loneliness. Although married couples share a home and often go on to have children together, there remains the sense that they often fail to connect in some way. While no marriage is represented as perfect, Hoonie and Yangjin and Isak and Sunja perhaps come closest. Entering into their marriages without expectations, they are pleasantly surprised by the qualities they discover in each other.

Names

The significance of names in Korean society is first illustrated when Sunja falls pregnant by Hansu. In the ensuing panic, much is made of the fact that Sunja's illegitimate baby will not be able to take the family name—a technicality which will make them both social outcasts. When Isak marries Sunja he saves her and the baby by giving him his family name—something of no consequence to him but of great significance to them. This scenario emphasises the way in which names can go a long way to defining an individual and their destiny.

Names are also significant in the context of Japan's oppression of the Korean people. The requirement that Koreans should have Japanese names on their identity papers is just one example of the way Korean cultural identity is quashed. Sunja feels her Japanese name (Junko Bando) has no connection to who she is. Noa, meanwhile, chooses to adopt his Japanese name at school— a sign of his futile wish to become Japanese.

Forced into adopting Japanese names, the Korean characters

81

assert what freedom they have when naming their children. Isak expresses his gratitude to his brother by asking him to name his sons. This tradition continues when Yoseb also goes on to name his great-nephew, Solomon. In each case, Yoseb chooses a name which he hopes will shape the child's destiny. Noa is named after the builder of the biblical ark in the hope that he will inherit his namesake's faith in the impossible. Solomon, meanwhile, is named after the wise man and king, reflecting Mozasu's hope that he will go on to become a great man of the world. As it turns out, neither one lives up to the promise of their names. Noa loses all faith in God and life itself while Solomon rejects an international lifestyle to follow in his father's footsteps. This demonstrates that, while names can aim to define a person, the success of this goal depends upon the will of the individual.

Beauty

During her marriage to Hansu, Mieko becomes accustomed to her husband's mistresses turning up on the doorstep. When Sunja appears asking for Hansu, however, Mieko judges that the woman at her door is not beautiful enough to fall into this category. Assessing Sunja's appearance harshly, she notes her rough hands and sees only vestiges of attractiveness in her. Still beautiful herself, thanks to a life of ease and comfort, Mieko would no doubt be dumbstruck if she learned that Sunja has been the woman who has occupied her husband's thoughts for many years.

Even in the prime of her youth, Sunja never meets the classical ideal of feminine beauty. Possessing "little delicacy in her face or limbs", she has strong hands and a sturdy body which is "built for hard work". Nevertheless, she immediately catches the eye of Hansu. For him, Sunja's beauty lies in the very areas which Mieko would dismiss as unfeminine. Attracted to the purposeful way she carries herself and her work-worn hands, he sees that much of Sunja's strength of character is expressed in her physical appearance.

Lacking any sense of vanity, even as a young woman, Sunja becomes even less concerned about beautifying herself as the years pass by—eschewing make-up and eventually having her hair cut short like a man's. Prematurely aged by hard work she, nevertheless, remains attractive. Sunja's physical appeal represents

the unflashy and often overlooked beauty of ordinary women—
providing a refreshing contrast to the images of perfection that
society so often equates with beauty. Shunning airbrushed
flawlessness, Min Jin Lee celebrates women whose life experiences
are written on their faces and bodies.

Food

Food is mentioned a great deal in *Pachinko* and, in the first section
of the novel, this is often in relation to its scarcity. From 1910 until
the 1950s, the Korean characters suffer from insufficient food
supplies. In Korea, this is the result of corrupt Japanese rule. In
Japan, it is the consequence of low pay and, later, the impact of
World War II upon the Japanese economy. For readers accustomed
to a surplus of available food, Lee's descriptions of privation are
thought-provoking. The scarcity of basic necessities is powerfully
brought home in the scene where Yangjin struggles to acquire a
small quantity of white rice to celebrate Sunja's marriage.

Throughout *Pachinko,* there is a strong association between
Korean women and food. For the earlier generations of women in
the novel, cooking is a way of nurturing their family but also
provides a chance for them to contribute to the family finances.
Creating delicious dishes provides an outlet for the female
characters' creativity and gives them an opportunity to demonstrate
their resourcefulness.

Yangjin's ingenuity at making delicious meals from sparse
ingredients plays a key role in the success of her boarding house.
Her reputation as a fantastic cook ensures that she always has a full
complement of lodgers and it is Yoseb's reports on her cooking
which initially draw Isak to the boarding house. In Japan, Sunja and
Kyunghee spend their days cooking together and eventually use
their culinary skills to build up a business making *kimchi* and other
side dishes. Although involving hard toil and the juggling of
childcare, the work gives both women a sense of agency and
empowerment.

In the final section of the novel, Lee illustrates how society has
changed when Sunja and Kyunghee learn, with astonishment, that
Phoebe's mother does not cook. A Korean-American, Phoebe has
been raised on fast food and has only ever tasted Korean food in
restaurants. While it is "inconceivable" to Sunja and Kyunghee

"that a Korean mother didn't cook for her family", Phoebe's mother is a career woman who does not have time to slave for hours in the kitchen. Proud of her inability to cook, she feels it signals her liberation from traditional female roles.

Clothes

When Sunja is young, her father tells her that what a man wears or possesses has "nothing to do with his heart and character." Nevertheless, clothes are described in *Pachinko* in considerable detail, and what the characters wear often reveals something about them (if only the things that they are trying to disguise.)

When Sunja first sees Hansu, it is his fine Western-style clothes that make him stand out. Despite her father's warning, she is impressed by how white and pristine Hansu's outfit is (particularly when compared to the filthy clothes of the Chung brothers, permanently imbued with a fishy stench). To Sunja, Hansu's immaculate clothes make him look like a movie star. To readers, however, they are a sign of his slippery nature. The fact that Hansu is a fish broker but has spotless hands and never smells of the product he trades in demonstrates that he gets others to do his dirty work (as is later illustrated when he uses Kim Changho as a front man). Years later, when Hansu turns up at Kim's restaurant, Sunja is to wonder how Hansu's shoes can be so shiny when there is no shoe polish available during the war. The answer is, of course, the black market and it is Hansu's lack of moral scruples that enables him to come out of any situation looking dapper and smelling of roses.

In Hideo Takano—the Japanese manager of Cosmos Pachinko—we see a similar preoccupation with sharp suits and shoes polished "to a mirror sheen." Although a very wealthy man, Takano has made his money from a business which is considered to be disreputable and usually dominated by Koreans. By dressing like an upmarket businessman, he glosses over the source of his wealth.

When Isak first appears at Yangjin's boarding house he also cuts an elegant figure in his smart Western-style clothes. In his case, however, his immaculate appearance reflects who he truly is. Isak can afford well-cut clothes as he comes from a wealthy family, but his pleasing appearance also reflects his temperament. A true gentleman who possesses great integrity, he never hits a false note in terms of behaviour or how he presents himself.

Isak passes on his high presentation standards to Noa who dresses immaculately even when he is a schoolboy living in the Korean ghetto. For Noa, presenting a smart exterior to the world helps him feel as if he is transcending his circumstances and achieving his aim of being a "good Korean". This goal, however, soon turns into a more dangerous desire to pass as Japanese. By contrast, Mozasu is uninterested in clothes and only submits to being fitted for good suits at Goro's insistence. More at ease with his identity than his brother, he sees no need to present an impressive exterior to other people.

When Sunja arrives in Japan, her traditional clothes mark her out as Korean, making her the target of hostile stares from the Japanese. While she eventually dresses to blend in, she has neither the inclination nor money to worry about fashion as her life is taken up with the practicalities of supporting her family. By the time she is in her sixties, Mozasu's wealth means that Sunja can wear French designer clothes and Italian shoes. Nevertheless, there is still the sense that she is dressing to fit in rather than for her own pleasure. Although adopting the costume of "a wealthy Tokyo matron", her prematurely aged skin gives away her history.

Pachinko

Lee's novel takes its title from the most popular arcade game in Japan. Similar to traditional pinball, the object of pachinko is to direct balls around a machine with the help of flippers. While the game involves a certain amount of skill, luck is also required. A player's chance of winning may also be skewed if the pachinko machine has been rigged. This practice is illustrated in *Pachinko* when Goro is shown bending a machine's pins by tapping them with a hammer. This changes the trajectory of the ball when the game is played.

Pachinko plays a large part in the fortunes of key characters in the novel. Mozasu and Noa both enter the pachinko business (Mozasu enthusiastically, Noa as a kind of penance) and make a great deal of money. At the end of the novel, Solomon also declares his intention to become involved in the business. While pachinko is shown to be one of the few routes to financial success for Koreans in Japan, it is a business that comes with a stigma attached. Avoiding breaking the laws against gambling through technicalities, pachinko occupies a moral and legal grey area. Lee demonstrates how the Japanese attitude to pachinko reflects the treatment of the Korean people generally. As the arcade game is big business and makes a significant contribution to the country's economy, it is not in the government's interest to ban it. Just as Koreans are never fully accepted as Japanese citizens, however, the pachinko parlours are not acknowledged as fully legitimate businesses.

On another level, the game of pachinko acts as a metaphor for the spirit in which the Korean characters live their lives. For many of them, it seems as if an invisible hand has tampered with the pinball pins at their birth, giving them little hope of winning. Nevertheless, they still have control of the flippers and, with skill and luck, victory is always a faint possibility. Mozasu is drawn to pachinko and understands the mentality of his clientele as it reflects his own philosophy on life— "his customers wanted to play something that looked fixed but which also left room for randomness and hope". It is this ability to lose but then return, hoping that the next game will turn out better, that has enabled his family to endure their many trials.

DISCUSSION QUESTIONS

1/ *Pachinko* tells the stories of a large cast of characters through an omniscient narrator. Why do you think the author chose a God-like, third-person narrator, and why so many characters? If you could have chosen to stay with just one character's perspective, who would it have been and why?

2/ The novel includes Korean and Japanese words without explaining their meaning. What impact did this have on your reading experience? Why do you think the author chooses not to include a glossary?

3/ Many of the characters in *Pachinko* are born into seemingly cursed circumstances—from Hoonie, who is born with physical disabilities, to Noa who is illegitimate. Discuss the various misfortunes that the characters are burdened with from birth. Do you think they are really doomed (like players in a Greek tragedy) or do they have some agency over their fates? How does the theme of curses link with Korean identity in general?

4/ When Sunja is still a teenager, Jun's wife offers up her rather depressing reflections on the destiny of women— "a woman's life is endless work and suffering" and "For a woman, the man you marry will determine the quality of your life completely." How true do these statements prove to be for Sunja and the other female characters of the novel? Do they suffer more than their male counterparts?

5/ Hansu is a morally ambivalent and intriguing character. What initially attracts him to Sunja and vice versa? How does he differ from Isak? Did your opinion of him change as the novel progressed?

6/ When Sunja first sees Hansu, she immediately notices his immaculate Western-style suit and white leather shoes. What do the clothes the characters wear reveal (or in some cases conceal) about them?

7/ *Pachinko* powerfully highlights the discriminatory nature of Japanese society. Discuss how prejudice impacts not only Koreans but also Japanese characters like Haruki, Risa, Etsuko and Hana. What impact does it have on their choices in life? How does it make them feel?

8/ The novel begins with the line "History has failed us, but no matter." How does this statement reflect the theme of resilience in *Pachinko*? Which characters demonstrate the most resilience? Who shows the least?

9/ "Home" is a particularly emotive concept for the Korean characters due to their migrant status in Japan and the troubled history of Korea. Discuss the main characters' differing attitudes towards home and belonging.

10/ Discuss the personal sacrifices made by Sunja, Yangjin, Kyunghee, Etsuko and Ayame. How do they compare to sacrifices made by male characters such as Isak, Sexton Hu and John Maryman? Which struck you as the most impressive? Are any of the characters rewarded for the sacrifices they make?

11/ In Isak and Yoseb, and Noa and Mozasu, Min Jin Lee illustrates how different siblings brought up in the same household can be. Discuss the differences (in personality and attitudes to life) between these two sets of brothers.

12/ Noa's story is the central tragedy of the novel and epitomises the conflicted nature of Korean identity. How did you feel about the choices he made? Is Noa a tragic victim or could he have overcome his circumstances?

13/ Discuss the role that pachinko plays in the fortunes of the main characters. How does the game act as a metaphor for the spirit in which the Korean characters live their lives?

14/ Lee paints an unromanticised picture of love and marriage in the novel, investigating the many different types of intimacy or understanding that may exist between spouses. Thinking of the married couples in the novel, discuss their different motivations for marrying. Which marriage did you feel was most successful and why? How do the marriages compare to the relationships in the novel based purely on passion?

15/ As well as celebrating the intensity of the parent-child bond, the author is brutally honest about the suffering that this relationship can bring to both parties. Discuss the various parent-child relationships in *Pachinko*. How do they demonstrate the force of parental love? In what way do children cause pain to their parents and vice versa? Did Lee's representation of the parent-child dynamic strike a chord with you?

16/ Sunja is faced with a number of difficult choices in the novel and her decisions are shown to catalyse disastrous events. Discuss the consequences of Sunja's actions when she a) refuses to become Hansu's mistress b) allows Hansu to pay for Noa's university fees and c) approaches Noa outside his workplace. Could Sunja have foreseen the consequences of her actions? What would you have done in her situation?

17/ Food is mentioned frequently in *Pachinko*, particularly in relation to the female characters who invariably source and prepare it. Why does food feature so heavily in the novel? Discuss the way that cooking becomes a tool of empowerment for Yangjin, Sunja and Kyunghee. How does the attitude of Phoebe's family (who are Korean-Americans) differ?

18/ When Hansu's wife, Mieko, comes face to face with Sunja she incorrectly concludes that the other woman is not beautiful enough to tempt her husband. What do you think the author wants to convey about concepts of female beauty?

19/ Towards the end of the novel, Solomon decides to split up with Phoebe, remain in Japan and exchange the world of international banking for pachinko. Why does he make this decision and how does it reflect his family's overall progress as Korean migrants in Japan?

20/ What did you make of the closing scene where Sunja visits Isak's grave? Did you consider this to be a bleak, or hopeful end to the novel?

21/ While describing the everyday lives of her characters, Lee conveys a great deal of historical and cultural background that readers may be unfamiliar with. What did the novel teach you about Korean and Japanese history? Did *Pachinko* change your perception of Korea and its people?

QUIZ QUESTIONS

1/ Hoonie is born with two physical deformities. What are they?

2/ What serious illness do Hoonie and Isak both contract?

3/ How does Sunja pay off Yoseb's debt to moneylenders?

4/ Why is Isak imprisoned in Japan?

5/ What is Noa's favourite type of reading matter?

6/ Why is Haruki's family forced to live in a slum area of Japan?

7/ How does Yoseb become horrifically burned?

8/ What happens to Bokhee and Dokhee after Yangjin loses the boarding house?

9/ How does Yoseb try to persuade Kim Changho to stay in Japan?

10/ As a teenager, Noa's wife, Risa, became a social outcast because of her father's actions. What did he do?

11/ How does Ayame discover that her husband, Haruki, is gay?

12/ Why does Mozasu's girlfriend, Etsuko, give up custody of her children?

13/ How does Hana die?

14/ What does Sunja bury by Isak's grave at the end of the novel?

15/ What surprising information does Sunja learn from the groundskeeper of the cemetery?

QUIZ ANSWERS

1/ A cleft palate and a twisted foot

2/ Tuberculosis

3/ She sells the gold watch that Hansu gave her to a pawnbroker

4/ His colleague, Sexton Hu, mouths the Lord's Prayer during compulsory worship at a Shinto shrine

5/ Nineteenth-century English novels

6/ Most Japanese landlords will not rent to them as they consider the learning disabilities of Haruki's brother to be a curse

7/ He is caught in the atomic bombing of Nagasaki

8/ They are offered factory jobs but Yangjin later comes to believe they were lured into working in Japanese military brothels

9/ Yoseb gives Kim his permission to marry Kyunghee once he is dead

10/ He accidentally killed two of his patients by administering the wrong drugs and then killed himself

11/ She sees him in the park having sex with another man

12/ After committing adultery, she has little legal chance of keeping them. She also wants to spare her children further shame

13/ From AIDS

14/ A photo keyring with pictures of Noa and Mozasu

15/ She learns that Noa regularly visited Isak's grave, even when he was in hiding

FURTHER READING

Free Food for Millionaires by Min Jin Lee

The Orphan Master's Son by Adam Johnson

The Calligrapher's Daughter by Eugenia Kim

Drifting House by Krys Lee

Human Acts by Han Kang

Please Look After Mother by Kyung-Sook Shin

Everything I Never Told You by Celeste Ng

Homegoing by Yaa Gyasi

The Leavers by Lisa Ko

The Sympathizer by Viet Thanh Nguyen

The Interpreter by Suki Kim

The Good Earth by Pearl S. Buck

FURTHER TITLES IN THIS SERIES

Alias Grace (Margaret Atwood): A Guide for Book Clubs

Beartown (Fredrik Backman): A Guide for Book Clubs

Before We Were Yours (Lisa Wingate) A Guide for Book Clubs

Big Little Lies (Liane Moriarty): A Guide for Book Clubs

The Book Thief (Markus Zusak): A Guide for Book Clubs

Commonwealth (Ann Patchett): A Guide for Book Clubs

Educated (Tara Westover): A Guide for Book Clubs

The Fault in Our Stars (John Green): A Guide for Book Clubs

Frankenstein (Mary Shelley): A Guide for Book Clubs

A Gentleman in Moscow (Amor Towles): A Guide for Book Clubs

The Girl on the Train (Paula Hawkins): A Guide for Book Clubs

Go Set a Watchman (Harper Lee): A Guide for Readers

A God in Ruins (Kate Atkinson): A Guide for Book Clubs

The Goldfinch (Donna Tartt): A Guide for Book Clubs

Gone Girl (Gillian Flynn): A Guide for Book Clubs

The Great Alone (Kristin Hannah) A Guide for Book Clubs

The Great Gatsby (F. Scott Fitzgerald): A Guide for Book Clubs

The Grownup (Gillian Flynn): A Guide for Book Clubs

The Guernsey Literary and Potato Peel Pie Society (Mary Ann Shaffer & Annie Burrows): A Guide for Book Clubs
The Heart Goes Last (Margaret Atwood): A Guide for Book Clubs

The Husband's Secret (Liane Moriarty): A Guide for Book Clubs

I Know Why the Caged Bird Sings (Maya Angelou): A Guide for Book Clubs

The Light between Oceans (M.L. Stedman): A Guide for Book Clubs

Lincoln in the Bardo (George Saunders): A Guide for Book Clubs

Little Fires Everywhere (Celeste Ng): A Guide for Book Clubs

My Brilliant Friend (Elena Ferrante): A Guide for Book Clubs

My Name is Lucy Barton (Elizabeth Strout): A Guide for Book Clubs

The Narrow Road to the Deep North (Richard Flanagan): A Guide for Book Clubs

The Paying Guests (Sarah Waters): A Guide for Book Clubs

The Secret History (Donna Tartt): A Guide for Book Clubs

The Storied Life of A.J. Fikry (Gabrielle Zevin): A Guide for Book Clubs

The Sympathizer (Viet Thanh Nguyen): A Guide for Book Clubs

The Underground Railroad (Colson Whitehead): A Guide for Book Clubs

BIBLIOGRAPHY

Min Jin Lee. *Pachinko*, Grand Central Publishing, 2017

Arifa Akbar. 'Pachinko by Min Jin Lee—everyday heroes.' *Financial Times*, February 24, 2017

Tash Aw. 'Pachinko by Min Jin Lee review – rich story of the immigrant experience.' *The Guardian*, March 15, 2017

John Boyne. 'Pachinko review: a masterpiece of empathy, integrity and family loyalty.' *The Irish Times*, August 5, 2017

Joe Fassler. 'What Writers Can Take Away From the Bible.' *The Atlantic*, December 20, 2017

Tim Marshall. 'Korea: A History Of The North-South Split.' Sky News, April 4, 2103

Kallie Szczepanski. 'Japan's Untouchables: The Burakumin.' Thought.co, May 23, 2018

Jonathan Soble. 'A Novelist Confronts the Complex Relationship Between Japan and Korea.' *The New York Times*, November 6, 2017

Liam Stack. 'Korean War, a 'Forgotten' Conflict That Shaped the Modern World.' *The New York Times*, Jan 1, 2018

Mike Sunda. 'Japan's Hidden Caste of Untouchables.' BBC News, October 23, 2015

www.minjinlee.com

ABOUT THE AUTHOR

Kathryn Cope graduated in English Literature from Manchester University and obtained her master's degree in contemporary fiction from the University of York. She is the author of Study Guides for Book Clubs and the HarperCollins Official Book Club series. She lives in the Staffordshire Moorlands with her husband, son and dog.

www.amazon.com/author/kathryncope

Made in the USA
Coppell, TX
16 September 2020